Here I Am

Here I Am

Learning

Along

the

Way

Terry Samala de Guzman

ISBN 978-0-692-10730-0 (print)
ISBN 978-0-692-10731-7 (ebook)

Cover design by Gabriel Melcher and Mayapriya Long
Cover photo by Terry Samala de Guzman
Text design by Bookwrights

Printed in the United States of America

Contents

Don't Overthink It

I started to write these stories prompted by my adult children teasing me about my approach to life's most challenging moments: "Don't overthink it."

My son would recall the time he was visiting from college while we were in the midst of preparing to move from the house we loved and lived in for 11 years. While he was helping me sort through his stuff he remembered saying, "I can now understand why it is difficult to move." He said that's when I put my hand on his shoulder in a loving gesture exclusive to mothers and sons, and said, "Oh my dear, don't overthink it!"

I explained that I didn't mean to minimize the challenge, but there are just moments when "overthinking it" is an exercise in futility. They encouraged me to write about the "bits of wisdom" that they've heard from me, insights that have become my life tenets.

When I started writing and reflecting, I rediscovered how life's trials and triumphs led me to develop my life tenets – insights that have helped me grow, thrive, endure and get to where I am. Terry met Terry again in my childhood, in my youth, in my adulthood, and I saw more clearly how I evolved over time and space.

It became clear to me that while on the surface, some of my life and work choices seemed audacious, I was simply moving forward, embracing new opportunities to grow and learn.

One of these opportunities was to work in an artistic environment at the Museum of Contemporary Art (MCA) in Chicago. I had no prior experience working in a museum and did not know anything about contemporary art. I was hired because of my successful record as a COO and as the manager of a significant construction project in New York City. I moved to Chicago in December 2014. Having heard of Chicago's harsh winters, I came equipped with winter gear fit for the tundra.

While I am no art scholar, I have great appreciation for it. I marvel at how a picture, a painting, a sculpture, a song, a poem, a dance, a novel, can make you smile, cry, feel good, feel sad, lift the soul. I am awed by the creative talent of people who generate this wonderful body of work. I admire their courage for self-expression. I am inspired by the impact of their work on others.

Growing up in the Philippines, my exposure to art was limited to my parochial school's theater productions and my mother's love for poetry. I was not exposed to anyone else with a deep appreciation for art in its pure form. We did not go to museums or study art history. Moving to New York marked my first serious introduction to the art scene, where I began to develop my appreciation for the value of art and its impact on mankind. Still, I was a distant observer, a fair-weather patron.

In the three years that I worked at the MCA, I met some of the great artists of our time and was exposed to retrospective exhibitions presenting an artist's representative works over an extended period. My colleagues, some of the most respected curators in the world, carefully select what works to present, creating a thoughtful and intentional environment for the audience to appreciate the artist's work. In this environment, I learned to believe that each and every one of us is born with an artistic bone but very few become aware of this gift, and even fewer find a way to cultivate and express it. This epiphany has inspired me to wonder what form of art I can use to express myself. OK–I know I don't have a musical bone, I don't have a drawing bone, I'm done with my performing bone, but I do love to write. And while I write business and work documents well and extensively, I have not used writing as a means for self-expression.

I have written this book in this context: to curate and share some touchstone stories of my life's work. This sounds so presumptuous; why would anyone be interested in *my* stories? I don't consider my life extraordinary. I grew up in a small island in the Philippines, had a normal education, got married to my college boyfriend, immigrated to America, found a job, earned an MBA, raised two kids, and built a career. Now in my "golden years," I am a married working woman with two grown children living a comfortable upper-middle class life.

Depending on how you look at it, what may be interesting is how I embraced life and dealt with whatever it brought and what I've learned along the way: tenets that I've developed to help me cope, thrive and succeed.

I did not allow the loneliness of growing up in my parents' difficult marriage to overshadow what I knew was their love for each other and for their children. I found my way to America, landing a job in one of the most respected companies in the world, and earning an MBA from one of the top 20 business schools. I recognized my need for work/life balance, searched for it, and found it. I've stayed happily married for more than four decades, built a successful career and raised two kind, independent and open-minded kids, who are now both making courageous work and life choices on their own. I survived cancer, the tragic loss of young loved ones, and unexpected career setbacks.

I've learned to believe that, ultimately, we can achieve success and happiness while being true to who we are, to our values and our aspirations. I've become an advocate for building a sustainable lifestyle, living within our means and doing what we can to make a difference in the world. My faith has grown in terms of humankind's ability to reinvent ourselves by simply starting from where we are, declaring our intentions to "the universe" and committing ourselves to this intention.

I've learned to embrace differences, and trust in the wisdom that comes from the heart to help navigate some of life's most complex developments. And while I continue to seek my greater purpose, I'm practicing what I believe to be my present purpose now: to become a good servant-leader, an available teacher-learner. I've learned to believe that perfection is the enemy of "good" and that good is good enough.

Life has presented me with many surprises, and while those are unique to me, despite our many differences—be it race, gender, religion, sexual orientation, or political beliefs, in our humanity we have so much in common. My hope is that telling my story will move others to find their voices and discover their pathway for true self-expression. I also hope the tenets I've distilled from each of my stories will benefit the younger men and women who are starting out in their lives and their careers. They are making difficult life choices while striving to live independently and find happiness and fulfillment. Don't overthink it. It is all about growing and learning.

So, here I am. I am no William Shakespeare or Maya Angelou, but this is my art, and this is my self-expression. Like any artist, I realize that my work could be a hit or a miss to those who experience it. But not to me. It is my art, and I am satisfied and grateful that I have completed it.

I do not know what the future holds; I only know that I am driven to continue to seek and fulfill my aspiration to add value, make a difference, create positive impact, and fulfill my purpose.

I have a paper weight on my desk, engraved with Ralph Waldo Emerson's famous quote:

"Do not go where the path may lead, go instead where there is no path and leave a trail."

Here I am. I have gone where there is no path, and this is my trail.

———

Go Where There is No Path and Leave a Trail.

———

Remember Where You Came From

We are all born to our circumstances. We don't get to choose our parents and relatives, our birthplace and early childhood experiences. And yet they all have lasting effects on how we develop and become the adults we are today. But we do have a choice about how we allow these circumstances to shape what and how we will become. We can choose to blame these circumstances for the rest of our lives or simply accept that they are part of who we are and learn to evolve to become the people we would like to be.

I was born in the town of Calapan, the island of Mindoro, located in the southern part of the Philippines. Having been born and raised Catholic, for me was not a choice, but a birthright. When I think of my childhood, my first clear memories are of being with my maternal grandfather and our dog, Master. My grandfather, "Tato," as we called him, was a gentle old man, who used to play tuba for the church choir. I have very fond memories of sitting with him, waiting for my mother to come home from teaching and watching with delight as Master ran off to meet her. I don't know why, but that memory is as clear as if it was yesterday. They were tender moments of care and affection. In many ways, it is unfortunate that in this day, age, and society, extended families rarely live together. Living with my maternal grandparents, especially Tato, was a special gift to me as a child. We didn't do anything special; he was too old to be even playful. But he was there, he was kind, and I knew he cared for me. That was plenty.

I am the youngest of four children, five to eight years after my siblings. So my brother and sisters all seemed much more grown up than me. I was the tag-along, sometimes the butt of their jokes, sometimes the pest. I was a precocious child, not to be dismissed, confident, and perhaps wiser than my years, even then.

My mother was a brilliant woman, a scientist who could explain any natural phenomenon to a curious child or an inquisitive adult. She was an avid reader and could recite from memory inspiring lines of poetry or famous quotes at any appropriate moment.

She was also a distant mother. She was not prone to show affection, hug, or kiss. I remember when I was about in my second grade, I went over to play at a friend's house and witnessed her mother hugging my friend when we arrived. It seemed to be such a nice ritual, and I wondered why we didn't do that in our house. I remember trying to have a conversation with my mother about a boy I was attracted to and she wouldn't hear about it, "You are too young and should not think of those things," she sternly reprimanded me. My mother created order in our lives. She was the epitome of strength and it seemed to me she could take on anything single-handedly.

This is probably because my father was mostly an absent father. He had enough independent means that he never had to work for anyone else, except to check on the land he inherited from his parents and the income it generated to support us, his family. Looking back, I think he must have been unbearably bored. So he drank, gambled, and womanized. When he was sober and around, he was a wonderful and fun father. My father was truly a paradox of a father. While he was mostly absent and preoccupied with having a good time instead of living up to the expectations of a responsible father, he redeemed these gaps with very memorable moments of sweet and clear demonstrations of love and attention. On my tenth birthday, he hand-carried a big birthday cake from the best patisserie in the Philippines. Years later, in another heroic fatherly act, he arranged that I be confirmed privately, with no less than the Bishop of the Catholic Church officiating and the Congressman of our province standing as my godfather. The bells tolled in my honor, and I kept thinking, *I wish my friends could see this!*

By the time I was seven, all my siblings had gone off to the city to study. Against this backdrop, I learned what it meant to grow up alone. Looking back now, this was the period in my life when I started to gain perspective. I learned empathy for my father's wayward ways—a product of his own absent parents. I learned resilience and self-reliance from my mother's no-nonsense ways —a product of her own poverty and her will to survive a difficult marriage. I began to understand how my mother had to make sure there was order in our home and that her kids were protected. My values and aspirations were being formed. I dreamt of having my own family and not becoming an absent or distant parent.

I found solace in going to school and immersing myself in extra-curricular activities. I was the youngest in every class – but this did not prevent me from becoming class president and graduating as the valedictorian in elementary and high school.

The rest of my childhood was defined by navigating through my parent's difficult marriage. I remember feeling very lonely, sad and helpless at home. Here I was, at the top of my class and leading all sorts of activities in school and there was nothing I could do to solve my parent's martial difficulties.

My children have wondered how I managed to grow up with positivity and optimism. I tell them that while my parents' relationship was far from ideal, and they could have certainly spared their children from the sadness of witnessing and growing up in their difficult marriage, I had no doubt that they truly loved each other and truly loved each and every one of their children. They also unquestionably encouraged and supported their children's interests, never putting any pressure on any of us to excel; and while unspoken, it felt like they were there, each and both of them, unconditionally for us.

And while I was born to circumstances that were not ideal and could have easily derailed me, I was lucky to realize that I didn't have to live under the shadow of these circumstances, and the lessons I've learned have steered me well. Growing up in a small town where everyone knew everyone grounded me. Losing my loving grandfather, Tato, when I was barely five years old taught me that time with people who matter to us is precious and fleeting, and we need to make the most out of our time together. My parents' difficult relationship gave me the resolve to become a more present life partner, a more demonstrative mother.

—

Growing up in a small town where everyone knew everyone grounded me.

—

Growing up in difficult family circumstances taught me that no matter what, knowing that you are loved is redemptive. This knowledge has given me the strength to evolve toward becoming the person I aspire to be, overcoming, and transcending my childhood circumstances.

Kids Learn from What You Do, Not from What You Say

My husband and I were born in the mid-1950s, part of the "baby boomer" generation. We were both born and raised in the Philippines and learned all the traditions and ways of its culture and society. Both of us were raised to be completely deferential to parental authority. We did as we were told. We both went to Catholic schools and observed Catholic traditions in families who were as God-fearing as they were law-abiding. We also both grew up in small towns and "what will people say" was how our mothers reminded us about proper behavior.

We met as blind dates in college, got married when I was 21 and he was 24 and immigrated together to America shortly thereafter, embracing the new culture that America offered us. We learned how to assert ourselves and became comfortable speaking even if not spoken to. We learned to behave based on our beliefs and values, and not for the sake of social acceptance. We moved away from being motivated by fear, and welcomed a more aspirational, positive approach to opportunities and challenges. Having both grown up in a homogenous society, we found and enjoyed new friendships from a diverse range of backgrounds. By the time we had kids, we had completely integrated into the American way of life. I was resolved to get parenting "right," but then soon realized that while many books have been written about how to be a good parent and raise successful children, parenting is a role that one simply takes on because it is far too complex to codify into a neat list of "how-tos". Kids learn from what you do, not from what you say, and the complexity of parenting increases when your children are growing up in a different context from the one you did.

What followed was our version of "Raising First Generation Americans 101," combining not only what we believed parenting should be, what we learned from our own family circumstances, but also what we liked in the Philippine culture and the American culture.

I was sure I didn't want to raise my kids in the traditional stereotypes of girls and boys. We did not paint our daughter's room pink, nor our son's room blue. Their toys included what they were drawn to—not just dolls for our daughter and cars for our son. They were equally exposed to sports and the arts; playing the piano and playing ball. Whether it was generational or cultural, one thing my husband and I feel we missed from how we were raised was the encouragement to "find our passion." So we supported the many trial-and-error activities to identify what this was for each of them. Our daughter discovered tennis; our son, the theater.

We were committed to ensuring we did not taint our kids with bias. It was a lesson I learned during my daughter's baptism, when, in his homily, the priest admonished the parents to not pass on their biases to their children. He reminded us that the children will have enough biases to deal with growing up, and they can certainly form their own, in their own time. This became one of my mantras as a parent.

When the kids were about eight and five, I had a casual conversation with both of them about sexuality. I explained that someday they will grow up and maybe have a family like ours, and although their mom is a girl and their dad is a boy, some families have two moms or two dads. And that is okay, too. I had gay friends at that time who were struggling to come out and I wanted our kids to understand early that our home is a safe environment for anyone to be open and true to themselves.

We had conversations about why I, their mother, worked in contrast to most of their classmates' moms who did not work. I explained that moms may choose to work because they like working, or sometimes, even if they don't like to work, financial reasons require them to do so. I said that in my case, it was both. I liked to work, and I needed to make money to help us afford our needs and wants in life. I reminded them that someday they can make the choice, and to remember that their partners in life can also make a choice.

We talked about money and the virtues of saving. I started to give them an allowance at age eight, and they both quickly learned that if they brought lunch from home, they can save their allowance to acquire some other fun thing. At around the same age, I got them both a loud old-fashioned alarm clock and gave them the responsibility of waking up on time to dress up, have breakfast, and catch the school bus. They also learned that homework was actually their *only* work, and they–not I–needed to get their homework done. That only when they really, really can't figure it out will I help. That if they don't do their homework and study, they take the risk of not advancing to the next grade. To this day, my now younger colleagues cannot comprehend how neither my husband nor I felt the responsibility to do our kids' homework.

When they became teenagers and started to spend more time alone with their friends, I thought it was important for them to understand and build confidence in their ability to exercise judgment. I said, "When you're at a party or somewhere with friends and there's something going on and you start feeling uncomfortable and thinking you shouldn't be there, that's the time to leave."

We continued to raise them in this bicultural household: semi-Filipino/semi-American. We traveled often to the Philippines to visit our family, and while they found some Filipino practices odd, they were more amused than horrified.

What we taught them and what they learned as bi-cultural, first-generation Filipino Americans, is now evident. Which things they choose to embrace, and which to leave behind are also becoming evident.

Raising kids in a bi-cultural environment is complicated.

They love Filipino food, not only because it is delicious but because we took every opportunity to sit down and eat together as a family. We regret we did not commit to their learning the Filipino language, Tagalog. While we were naturally drawn to a close circle of friends from diverse backgrounds, we wish they had a deeper understanding of the Filipino culture, and now wonder if we fell short by not developing stronger ties with Filipino communities. And while we know, and they'd say they believe in God, they are no longer practicing Catholics.

Pleasing our parents always weighs heavily on all of us. My husband and I were sure that if there was one thing we wanted to be clear about, it was that both our kids had the capacity and ability to define what success meant to them, authentically. So when they both went off to college—a true rite of passage in any culture—we shared with them what we called our three measures of success: complete college in four years, be able to support yourself after college, and be law-abiding (do not end up in jail). They have now met these measures. Beyond this, we continue to encourage them to discover and pursue what success and happiness mean to them and to find work that aligns with their values.

Raising kids is complicated; doing so in a bi-cultural environment raises this complexity a notch. We wrote our own parenting rules based on what we learned as children, and what evolved as our sense of values and moral compass. Our kids, first-generation Filipino Americans, are a product of this self-taught labor of love. And they turned out okay.

Our marriage, far from perfect, also turned out fine. While longevity is not necessarily the true measure of a successful marriage, four decades is noteworthy. We have learned to transcend our expectations of each other, enabling us to embrace our individual frailties, forgive our differences, and endure our shortcomings. We have been able to thrive, individually, and together, while building mutual trust and respect for each other. We got married so young that we feel we grew up together, learning that while we can argue wholeheartedly, sometimes, being kind is better than being right. We found out that almost always, a healthy dose of good humor works to diffuse heated disagreements.

—

Sometimes being kind is better than being right.

—

My husband and our kids have become the fertile soil from which I've grown and thrived. And, while arguably, I tended each of them with love and affection, I would not be where I am without them. My husband has been my anchor, and our kids, my sail. He has helped me remain grounded, and our kids have inspired me to move forward. We–each of us and the extended family we are becoming–have learned to grow our love for each other alone, as well as together. I am now learning from our grown children; my tenet that kids learn from what you do, not from what you say, has come full circle.

Step Forward When You're Called

I learned the important lesson of stepping forward to embrace unexpected opportunities and discover the essence of excellence from our school principal, Sister Merita.

A big woman with a big presence, she was a scholar of world history and a patron of the performing arts. Rumor had it that she came from Austrian royalty. I was in sixth grade when she arrived on the scene to take on the role of Mother Superior (or Principal) for Holy Infant Academy, the small parochial school I was attending in my native town and island. She brought with her a passion and energy that I have not witnessed before, launching a string of what we'd now call initiatives–initiatives that transformed our little school and shaped my growing mind.

She cast me in the lead role of "Snow White" in the first of her series of theater productions intended to raise funds for the school. The circumstances leading up to my selection were precarious and I learned many a life-lesson from this experience. Here's the scenario: it was an "operetta" and we, some of the chosen elementary kids, were members of the "background cast"–fairies or creatures of the forest. All the characters with speaking parts had been cast and taken by high-schoolers. Two weeks before opening night, we were in the midst of rehearsals, and Snow White couldn't remember her lines. Sister Merita was obviously not pleased, and as Snow White stuttered, the entire cast, especially the grade-school creatures of the forest, felt the intensity of the moment. Sister Merita turned around, surveyed the rest of us, pointed her finger at me, and hollered, "You!"

It could very well be the first time that I wondered aloud, "Me?"

"Yes, you," she said. "Come over here and read these lines." I stepped forward.

Soon-to-be-axed Snow White was understandably red with embarrassment. We could all have heard a pin drop. Without hesitation, I read the lines. "Good," she said, "Come to my office." Then declared, "We will resume rehearsal tomorrow."

I don't know or remember when she told former Snow White that she no longer was in the play, but I remember walking into her office for the first time wondering what's next. By now, fear, anticipation and, admittedly some level of excitement, were running high in my ten-year-old heart.

She commanded me to sit down and asked me to read a few more lines. Then she opened the script, picked a few pages, and told me, "I'd like you to memorize these lines for tomorrow's practice." She continued, "You are now Snow White."

It seemed to me that I all of a sudden grew older at that moment. It was a bag of mixed feelings: I felt awful for the Snow White I just replaced–she was really nice, and I thought I would never want to be in that situation of being humiliated and embarrassed for not being prepared. I felt some resentment for Sister Merita–she seemed merciless to replace a cast member that way; but I also felt awe for her swift decision and action. Then there was this spring of a new self-awareness about some capability that I did not know I had. I came home, shared the news with my mother, who was nonplussed about it, and I devoted the rest of the afternoon and evening memorizing the lines Sister Merita commanded me to memorize. The following day, I delivered the lines without missing a beat, and without much of a choice, I was thrown into this first important, unexpected role. I embraced the opportunity wholeheartedly. I memorized my lines, practiced religiously, and I debuted as Snow White to a happy audience. You may be wondering if I can sing too. No, I can't. It was the magic of lip-synch; backstage was a young nun with a beautiful operetta voice.

There was this spring of a new self-awareness about some capability that I did not know I had.

Sister Merita became a force in my life. From age ten to age fourteen, when I graduated from high school, she led the school and continued to produce school plays, with me in lead roles. In many ways, the theater became a respite for me–a place to get away from the loneliness of my life at home.

This school, under Sister Merita's leadership, was my go-to place. I was thriving in the theater, overall academically, and was a student leader. I was also having fun. We were a co-ed school, and by the time I was a junior, I had a great mix of girl and boy chums, and to this day, I look back to this period in my life with warm fondness.

By the time I was a senior in high school, I was clearly spending more time in my extra-curriculars than in studying. I was sure that one of my bright classmates was getting higher grades than me. I was still vying to graduate as the class valedictorian, but I was no longer sure if my academic standing was secure. Nor did I think I cared. I was having fun.

The tradition was for the principal, my beloved Sister Merita, to call in the top three graduating students to her office a couple of weeks prior to graduation to tell them their class ranking. I was one of those called in, and I walked in with the expectation that she would tell me I was # 3, or at best, #2. When she told me I was graduating as the class valedictorian, I burst into tears.

"Why are you crying?" she asked me.

I replied in disbelief, "I just didn't expect this. I knew my grades have slipped because I've been spending my time organizing and leading activities."

She grasped both my shoulders, held my gaze, and said, "I would like you to remember this: this honor is a symbol of excellence in a student. In this case, excellence is not narrow–it is multi-faceted, and you have exhibited excellence, serving as a role-model for your classmates."

Excellence is multifaceted.

I still don't know if my GPA was lower than the one who turned out to be #2, but this is a lesson in excellence I've taken with me.

It is incredible how the unlikely figure of a German nun assigned to run a small parochial school in the Philippines could have such a profound impact on my growth and development as a person. But this was Sister Merita's gift to me: she called on me to step forward into a lead role that taught me I can handle unexpected opportunities. She also helped me understand the essence of excellence.

Lead With Your Values

In a similar way to how my grade school principal made me step forward and thrust me into a lead role at age 10, I was thrust into the role of a team leader within a year of joining American Express.

My six-person "team" consisted of my former peers: four men—a Jewish guy from Brooklyn, an African American from the Bronx, a Trinidadian from Queens, a Puerto Rican from Staten Island; and two women—a Colombian-American from New Jersey and a Jamaican-American from Manhattan. Here I was, not only the youngest and newest among them, an immigrant never exposed to diversity, now tasked to become their boss. My first thought was that none of them could be happy about this. Sure, I'm likeable—but, really, to become their boss? The men were big and self-assured; the women were savvy and assertive. I thought if I were in their place, what would I want my new "boss" to do first? I spoke with each of them privately. I said, "Look, I am very happy about my promotion, and I don't know how you feel. I'm thinking you don't like this idea, but since we need to work together, all I'm requesting is that we respect each other. I have a lot to learn, probably from you, and if and when I do something that does not sit well with you, please tell me, in private. And I will do the same with you." Respect became our first unspoken rule.

—

Respect became our first unspoken rule.

—

A few months later, we were all working late on a monthly closing, in which we consolidated all of American Express's worldwide financial reports. The night was going slow and long, each of us waiting for reports from all over the world. Now just imagine this: our cubicles were arranged in a double-row fashion (typical of early 1980s office design), and as the supervisor, I took the last cubicle at the end of the row. Sitting across from me was our most senior accountant (let's call him John). One of the other guys (let's call him Roger) liked to chat on the phone. Roger was chatting away when I heard John call out, "Hey Roger, are you done with your work? 'Cause I don't understand how you could find time to be talking on the phone." Roger said something under his breath. It was inaudible to me but apparently not to John, because before I fully realized what was going on, these two men were up on their feet, face to face, yelling at each other, ready to punch each other out.

Pure instinct: I jumped to my feet, stood between them, and with both of my arms stretched out between them, shouted, "Stop!" I then looked at each of them and calmly said, "You can go home if you are tired, but if you need to stay, I ask you not to behave like this!" They both huffed and went back to their desks. The rest of the evening was quiet though I felt like I was sitting at the edge of my chair. I also made sure that one of them left earlier than the other, warning them that this squabble could not continue.

The following day, I reported the incident to my boss. He was incredulous, saying, "Geez Terry, those are two big guys (both were at least 6'2 and 180 pounds). It didn't occur to you that they might have started punching each other and you'd get hit?"

He was right, but of course that hadn't even crossed my mind. My instinct was simply to do the "right thing." I suppose that was my initiation to conflict resolution. I don't know if my boss wrote them up or reported them to HR. I didn't. John, Roger and I never spoke about the incident again, and while Roger's bad work habits eventually affected his work performance and John moved up in the organization, my sense is we all walked away from that incident with some important lessons learned on how we needed to behave with each other.

Becoming a good leader is not very different from becoming a good parent or building a good marriage. It requires a lot of work, a lot of self-reflection, and many sacrifices for the greater good. Recognition in the work place is mostly attributable to major achievements. In my case, the timely completion of projects, the successful closing of a major deal, the seamless integration of complex systems, building strong teams and keeping the organization in solid financial and operational footing. I've learned to believe that a good leader comes of age by being able to make good judgments.

—

A good leader comes of age by being able to make good judgments.

—

The rudiments of work become academic: you get it done. You are trained, you have experienced staff. A leader is often called upon to make difficult decisions in the face of ambiguity, when information is incomplete, and it boils down to a judgment call.

Letting people go, telling them they no longer have a job, is for me the most painful and difficult experience as a leader. No matter what the circumstances are–organizational changes that eliminate a position, incompetence, even real transgressions–the reality is that my decision, no matter how justified, is changing the course of the life of that person. A friend of ours, a famous surgeon, told us during his retirement dinner how he readied himself for surgery. He spoke of the preparation he went through the night before, and the care with which he performed the surgery itself. I feel letting someone go is akin to surgery. You are cutting through the person's skin, he/she will definitely bleed, and you need to make sure you handle it with such precision and care that there is some confidence that the bleeding will stop and with time, the person will return to good health, although it will take time.

Despite the pain of having to let some people go, what keeps me coming back to a leadership role is the opportunity to organize people towards the completion of a common goal and seeing them flourish on their own. Not unlike a teacher who hears from a student of long ago, I am always thrilled to hear from those I've led and to learn of their successes and achievements.

I've risen to high levels in the organizations where I've worked and many people have asked me how I deal with power.

I respect power. I am humbled by power. I take it very seriously that what I say or do, no matter how small, can have a ripple effect. My goal has become not only to deal with every person fairly but also respectfully–to include, not exclude; to be accessible, not distant; to be kind and generous, not self-serving.

—

I am humbled by power.

—

The truth is, I never really dreamed of becoming a leader. But somehow, I've found myself in that role. My journey as a leader has taught me that no matter what our differences are, we can achieve authenticity and success by finding common ground through the universal values of respect, integrity, trust, and humility.

This is what I believe my work as a leader was about. I've aspired to build an inclusive work place respectful of differences, a transparent organization founded on trust, and a world-class institution proud of its successes while humble in its imperfection. My hope is that my values will lead me to make a difference in my workplace and in the lives of the people I work with.

It's OK Not to be the Smartest in the Room

I've learned to believe that humility is one of the most important attributes of a good leader, and every aspiring leader would benefit greatly from the experience of being humbled.

My first humbling experience came when I was entering college, wherein I learned it's OK not to be the smartest in the room.

I was used to being the smartest and most confident kid in the room. My three siblings were much older than me, and I learned early on to be independent, assert myself, and get my way. While I was always the youngest in my class, I did not think it was a big deal that I graduated from elementary school at ten and from high school at fourteen, both times as class valedictorian. It was just what I did. I was also president of the student council, the theater club, the science club, as well as class president.

There was no question that I was going to college in the big city, as my older siblings had done before me. I knew exactly where I wanted to go: St. Theresa's

College (STC), a small all-girls liberal arts college in the Philippines. While I didn't personally know anyone who went there, I had heard about how progressive it was and how smart the kids were. I wanted to go where the smart ones went.

In the culture that was the Philippines in the early 70s, franchise over the higher schools of learning was held by the Catholic priests and nuns. Most, if not all, the schools catered to the upper class and were not co-ed. Thus, most of these schools were proudly hailed as "exclusive" by those who attended them. STC was also known for cutting through the social classes, rejecting the dominant "dumbed down" culture that valued how rich you are, what your daddy does, where you go on vacation, or how pretty and expensive your clothes are. Despite the narrow, homogenous lens of college life in the Philippines in the 70s, the environment at STC uniquely qualified as diverse and inclusive, another reason why I really wanted to go there.

Anyway, without even having stepped on the campus, I applied only to STC. Back then, all valedictorians were offered automatic admissions to all colleges in the Philippines, except STC, which required both an entrance exam and a merit scholarship exam. I passed the entrance exam but failed the merit scholarship exam. I had never failed a test. How could this be? I was shocked, disappointed, and ashamed. In my fourteen-year-old state of mind, all of a sudden, I was wondering if I was not as smart as I and everyone else thought.

Undeterred, I enrolled, rationalizing that it was just a fluke. I would show them. My IQ test landed me in the "high IQ" class, a cohort of some 30 supposedly very smart girls. While the results of the scholarship test were never published, I was sure some of these girls passed the scholarship test that I had failed. I was with the crème de la crème, and, for the first time in my life, I had this uncomfortable feeling that I wasn't the smartest anymore. At fourteen, I was also the youngest, with classmates at least two to three years older than me. They were not only smarter than me, but they also seemed so much more sophisticated and confident. I grew up in a small town and felt socially inept in this city environment.

In class, I was not failing, but I was not excelling at the level I was used to. I was working harder than I ever had but was no longer a straight A student. I auditioned for a theater production and didn't make the cut. While I thrived at being a student leader back home, I did not find the nerve to even think about it here.

Around the middle of my freshman year, I developed digestive problems caused by stress. While I thought my new college friends were much smarter and sophisticated than me, I discovered that they were also very kind, and they rallied for me. While I felt getting B's in math was a failure, they assured me that was pretty good. They helped me with homework. Some of them are still my closest friends.

Throughout my first year, I felt like I was treading water, and while my friends were holding my hands, I was still very scared of how deep the bottom was. My parents were very supportive. They never made me feel that they were in any way disappointed. They helped me seek medical attention, and I recovered. The idea of dropping out from this demanding program and difficult transition never occurred to me. Somehow, I believed–or convinced myself–that I'd get through it. And I did. After I survived my first year, I found my footing, and regained my self-confidence. Henceforth, my less-than-stellar grades were not because I couldn't cope, but because I found a diversion in college weekend parties. Let's just say I found a happy balance between studying and partying. Graduating at the top of my class was no longer a goal. It would have taken too much work, I wasn't even sure it was achievable, and spending time with my college classmates and friends was far more fun than studying harder anyway. I was learning so much more about life. I graduated in four years, at age eighteen, with a respectable "B" GPA, arguably a solid "A" anywhere else.

In retrospect, college taught me some very important life lessons. Failing the scholarship test was my first humbling lesson. I learned that I had been living in a small bubble in my small town and my small school, and that transitions can be difficult and stressful. I learned that stress can make one sick, and that one must pay attention to the symptoms and seek help. I learned the value of supportive parenting and being there for your child, unconditionally. I learned what it means to have strong, smart, and kind friends. I learned about the meaning of trade-offs and balance.

Finally, I was humbled into finding out that I did not have to be the smartest one, and that was OK.

Start from Where You Are

In my work as a life coach, many clients come to see me with a deep longing to reinvent themselves. And instead of asking them what they'd like to become, I ask them about their skills, their core competencies, *now*. We need to start from where we are. I learned the truth of this myself over time, and the lessons unfolded from my first job out of college in the Philippines and later on, from my first job as a young immigrant in the US.

I was about to graduate from college and eager to land a job. The only problem was that I was about to graduate with a degree in accounting, and I did not want to work as an accountant. In fact, I did not want to become an accountant at all. My mother somehow influenced me into believing that my initial preferences–psychology or foreign service–would lead to unemployment; that a business degree would make me employable, and an accounting degree would be even better. I got the degree but refused to become an accountant. I think I had bought into the bias that accountants were boring, narrow-minded introverts with no imagination and zero personality. So when my father asked me if he could introduce me to one of his friends, a partner in one of the top accounting firms, I politely declined. I said I'd prefer to find my job on my own.

Two weeks before my college graduation, I ran into a friend who mentioned that his boss was looking for an assistant, and he would be happy to make the introduction. This boss seemed to have his fingers on the pulse of what was going on in the Philippines at that time. The job was to assist him in two of his professional roles: Special Advisor to the Chairman of the Board of the Development Bank of the Philippines and President of the Rotary Club.

Of course, at that time, I had no idea what all this meant. But I was impressed by what I saw. My would-be office was on the top floor of a swanky office building. Up there, the sweeping views of the city were breathtaking. The walls were beautifully paneled in mahogany, the floors were sparkling parquet and marble, and you could hear and feel the doors slowly close air-tight. It not only felt glamorous; it felt like important things happened here. This was not the cubicle farm where every fresh graduate at that time landed.

I applied for the job and got it. Here's how I saw it: it was not an accounting job, and I was going to work for one of the up-and-coming executives in the Philippines. I did not see any downside. Besides, I was eighteen years old. I was just going with the flow.

On my first day on the job, I quickly realized I did not know what an administrative assistant does. I had never worked in an office, did not know the protocol for taking calls, and I simply did not have the wherewithal for all the tasks that any boss would assume an admin assistant would cover.

My boss was a good teacher. One day, he walked in while I was taking a call for him, and he coached me about the protocol for receiving calls. He taught me one lesson that has served me well ever since: "Anticipate your boss' needs."

—

Anticipate your boss' needs.

—

Somehow, I figured things out, ran the office well, but I was also quickly finding out that I did not want to continue to work as an admin assistant. It just wasn't a good fit for me. That was when I started studying for my CPA exams. Why? Why not? I took the exams and passed.

My boss' star was rising and he had just launched a consulting company and I thought there might be an opportunity there for a new CPA, like me. Curious, I started to ask my new colleagues in the consulting company questions about what they do. Is it interesting? Is it fun? I got curious to the point that I asked my boss if I could transfer over to the consulting team and become what was then a "junior analyst." He was offended, asking, "Don't you like working for me? Don't you realize how much access you have to me, a privilege on its own?" Maybe this was my first attempt at diplomacy, as I explained to him that he needed a more deserving assistant. It was clear to me, and I'm sure obvious to him, that I did not have the training nor the competencies for the kind of assistant that he needed. I declared my gratitude to him and my sincere appreciation for everything I had learned from him.

I got the promotion. Six months after my college graduation, I moved on and took on the title "junior analyst" at one of the most prestigious companies in the Philippines. I had just turned 19. Clearly my accounting education had prepared me well to analyze financial statements and provide financial projections for clients. I started to appreciate accounting. I met accountants who were interesting, fun, smart, and creative. Maybe I'd become an accountant after all.

By the time I immigrated to the US, I had work experience in finance and accounting at two of the most prestigious companies in the Philippines. It was 1979, the dawn of the computer age, and one of my work experiences was leading the conversion of a manual general ledger system into a computerized system. I had become a fully-fledged accountant.

The reality however, is that none of my background meant much in America. No one understood the context that I studied from the same books and curricula as any accredited college here and that my professors were educated in some of the top business schools in the US. Aside from curiosity, no one was really interested in the companies I had worked for in the Philippines. There was no malice associated with this lack of interest or regard. Put simply, the absence of context made it seem irrelevant. It happens all the time: we have no doubt all spoken to a cab driver or store vendor with a thick accent and learned that he was an engineer or a teacher back home.

So, while I was lucky to have landed a job at American Express in New York City, it quickly became clear to me that the college degree, CPA, and work experience I brought from the Philippines meant nothing in New York's financial district. I soon realized that to remain competitive and qualify for promotional opportunities, I needed to gain additional local (US) credentials to strengthen my credibility as a professional. In order to gain confidence and feel I belonged in this environment, I had to reinvent myself. But where to begin?

—

I had to reinvent myself. Where to begin?

—

It was 1980 and the buzz among my young ambitious colleagues was business school. An MBA. I decided this was how I'd build my local credibility—earn my MBA.

The first step was to take the GMAT, a standard test to see if you were smart enough to handle graduate school. Although I didn't realize then that your GMAT score was the gating factor for placement in the top business schools, I found out that you could prepare for the GMAT with a practice test book. I stopped by a bookstore, purchased the book, and spent many weekend hours taking the practice tests. One hot summer day, I found myself in a big high school gym somewhere north of New York City where I took the GMAT.

I was naively unbiased for or against any business school. My priority was simple: to find a school that offered the most convenience for navigating my commute: a short walk from work, on to my homeward bound train. I'd be taking evening classes, while continuing to work full time like many/most of my classmates, and efficiency was paramount. I looked at the business schools in lower Manhattan. Only one school qualified: the New York University Business School (now Stern, which at that time was located on Trinity Place).

Little did I know that this step would become a defining moment, both for my life as an immigrant and for my career development. I wish I had kept a record of my GMAT score, as I have no recollection of what it was. I wish I had kept a copy of my application form, to see what a 24-year-old immigrant had to say about her interest in an MBA. I learned later that I had applied to and was accepted by one of the most prestigious business schools in the world. Getting in–not to mention finishing–did in fact establish my professional credibility and helped open many doors for me.

While I achieved my goal of completing an MBA, the valuable lessons I learned extended well beyond the classroom. What mattered the most was not learning how to value a stock or create a business plan. I figured out how to survive and thrive in a demanding academic environment and maintain the grade point average required to stay in the program, while also actively advancing my career and my life goals. I learned how to make time for family and friends and make clear priorities. Those grueling years in grad school taught me how to finish what I started and the value of reinventing one's self. Something in me knew to start with my existing competencies and experience. It was not evident at the time how things would play out for me, but I evolved.

Finding my first job out of college, rebelling against the concept of becoming someone I thought I did not want to become actually led me to my first major lesson in career navigation, and the importance of finding work that authentically resonates with my sense of self. In retrospect, I can see it seriously changed my life. I figured out how to make things work, experiment, take risks, discover and learn. I made it work. I learned to embrace my excellent training and competent skills in accounting, applying them in ways I knew were not only practical, but creative.

And while I did not set out to intentionally realize my childhood aspiration to work as a diplomat or a counselor, my work as an accountant—eventually becoming a Chief Financial Officer—opened doors for me to teach global leadership to MBA students and executives. I've also become a certified executive coach, helping clients navigate through their work/life challenges and opportunities.

Despite my bias against accounting, it became obvious that the credential was a strategic advantage because it gave me a place from which to grow. Just as I advise my coaching clients now, building on my core training and competency led me, may I dare say, to a very interesting career path.

When You Discover the World, You Discover Yourself

My career path and life became more interesting when I immigrated to America. I wish I could cite a noble reason for coming to America. I did not come because I was being persecuted in my native country. I did not come to find freedom or a safe haven, nor was I searching for a "better" life. While I appreciated America's fundamental promise of life, liberty and the pursuit of happiness, I came simply because I was young, feeling carefree, and looking for adventure. I was 24, living a comfortable life and building a promising career in the Philippines.

My older sisters had immigrated to the US in the late 70s. While immigration to the US is a much more complicated and trying process now, it was relatively much easier then. The US was trying to attract talent, and my oldest sister, a chemical engineer, simply applied for an immigrant's visa and got approved. A few years later, she petitioned for us, prompted by my parents' desire to have an option to flee the Philippines during President Marcos' regime.

I came to the US to claim my green card and went back to the Philippines after a couple of months. I felt compelled to stay in the Philippines with my parents as they aged. While my older siblings had moved permanently to the States, my parents chose not to do so. They enjoyed their independent life in the Philippines and were content to visit my siblings and their families once a year, and that seemed sufficient to fill the gap of days and miles of separation.

It didn't take long for me to feel that America seemed to be calling me to come back. The change of seasons appealed to me and I loved how fashion changed with the seasons. I was fascinated by the diverse faces of people on the street and intrigued by how anyone and everyone could blend into the backdrop and become invisible. I wanted to experience living this way but did not think I'd stay longer than a couple of years. I figured I'd find a job, go to grad school, travel some, and then come back to the Philippines.

Have you ever been faced with a difficult decision without any confidence in a clear outcome?

I felt very conflicted between what I felt I wanted to do (come to America) and what I felt I should do (stay in the Philippines).

I prayed. I consulted with trusted advisors and heard comforting words: "Your parents aren't really old yet... you can always visit." I also heard, "They would love if you stayed...you will be too far away." My parents did not try to influence or pressure me in one way or the other.

—

Have you ever been faced with a difficult decision, without any confidence in a clear outcome?

—

I decided to return to America. While I missed my parents, friends, and the familiarity of everything that was my life for 24 years, I discovered a life in America that I really liked. My husband and I both found good jobs and new friends. We both relished the sense that we were building a life together. While I missed my parents, I enjoyed being near my siblings and their young children. We learned that many opportunities that were out of reach for us in the Philippines were within reach for us here. We were able to save, secure a mortgage, and buy our own house within two years. At the end of our second year we visited the Philippines, and came back to America–this time, to stay.

The search for adventure that brought us to the US led us to a way of life uniquely American: open and welcoming, competitive and progressive, kind and generous. We built very fulfilling and rewarding lives for ourselves, giving birth to and raising our two children here. We now hold dual citizenships, and when asked if I feel like an American or a Filipino, I say both. I honestly do feel that way. Through the years, we have made it a point to visit the Philippines regularly, so that our children are very familiar with the Philippine culture. We have managed to stay connected with relatives and old friends in the Philippines in the same way that we have been able to develop long-standing friendships here. We have figured out how to be faithful dual citizens of the two countries we deeply love. We now call both countries "home."

My perspective on America has shifted from a fascination for "adventure land" to a deep admiration, love, and respect for a special place that has prevailed in its commitment to democracy, in providing a safe haven for the citizens of the world, and in offering opportunities openly and equally to anyone and everyone.

While the current political narrative refers to building walls and America continues to struggle with racial divide and political strife, my faith in this country is unshaken. I believe that it will sustain its place in the world as the proverbial land of freedom. I believe it will remain faithful to its promise of welcoming immigrants, a place where an immigrant like me could find her way to build a life, a good life, a free and happy life.

My hope is that people like me–immigrants–who leave their native homes to live in a foreign land, ultimately find this new sense of welcome and belonging.

—

America is great.

—

Moving to America encouraged us to discover the rest of the world. A year after we arrived, we booked a European tour. Never mind that we spent most of our fourteen days on a bus crisscrossing through Europe. We caught a glimpse of London, Paris, Innsbruck, Lausanne, Munich, Florence, Rome, Venice, and Amsterdam. We saw the Mona Lisa and the Pietà for the first time, prayed at St. Peter's Basilica, gazed at the Eiffel Tower, witnessed the changing of the guard at Buckingham Palace, rode a gondola in Venice, and marveled at Amsterdam's flower market. We took pictures of cherished sights, places we'd happily go back to for a longer stay.

I read that one of the benefits of traveling is that you are not surrounded by the same old furniture that you own that you know you cannot afford to change. When you travel, you are surrounded by things you haven't seen, people you haven't met, and places you haven't been. All your senses experience a kind of awakening. Your entire being goes through the novelty of an experience that is energizing and exciting. I've learned to feel that and now I get a giddy feeling when I'm airborne, looking out on to the clouds, imagining a life beyond.

—

When you travel all your senses experience a kind of awakening.

—

Over the years, we've returned to some of the places we caught a glimpse of during our first European bus cruise and have since discovered new ones. We introduced our children early to traveling. Some of the trips were to visit our native country, the Philippines, but we also indulged in more extensive explorations.

When I turned 50, we took a glorious cruise through the Mediterranean. While we each have our own special memories from this trip, one that I hold dearly was our daily afternoon gathering at our cabin's outside deck for cocktails and snacks. I consider myself an amateur photographer and some of my best pictures date back to this trip. I wrote extensive journals. I watched the sun rise and set with the endless sea as a backdrop. I had been diagnosed with breast cancer just prior to this trip, and I felt that this trip prepared me well for what was to come.

Six years later, I celebrated my "full remission" with another trip–this time, alone, to Nepal. No, I did not hike or climb. I simply immersed myself in the spirituality of Nepal. While I was initially shocked by the poverty all around me, I learned to appreciate the deep faith that the people of Nepal shared, regardless of differences in their religious beliefs. I strolled around Lake Pokhara on a moonlit night and felt in my heart the deepening of my own faith.

Yes, travel provides spiritual renewal. Being in places like Lake Pokhara, the Grand Canyon, the Grand Tetons, Yellowstone National Park, the Canadian Rockies; sailing on the great seas like the Mediterranean, the Adriatic; witnessing sunrises and sunsets in Bali, Dubrovnik, or Rio de Janeiro; beholding the natural order of life in the great safari parks of Kenya and South Africa; walking onto rainbows and getting drenched in Victoria Falls. All of these experiences have moved me into feeling I was in God's presence. Engaging in diverse cultures has also instilled in me a stronger faith in the human spirit and our innate ability to transcend and overcome differences and difficulties.

—

Travel provides spiritual renewal and strengthens one's faith in the human spirit.

—

My husband and I have now committed to a "bucket list" and one of our items is to visit a new place every year: a place we haven't been that for some reason or another holds curiosity and mystery for us. Our record has been good, and we will continue as long as we can afford to do so, physically and financially. It has become a priority for us. We live a comfortable life, not luxurious. We don't need fancy cars and homes, but travel, we must. We'll see how far we get.

While the Western culture measures growth and success vertically according to the proverbial ladder of success, I understand the Native Americans measure one's progress like the layers of the rings in the trunk of a tree. This is what traveling does for me. It allows me to grow and build layers of wisdom and knowledge that makes me whole and strong. Climbing a ladder presents a danger of falling, while adding layers of rings simply takes time, care, and the will to keep going.

Leaving the comforts of home started as an adventure. It led to a gut-wrenching choice to immigrate to America. My move to America introduced me to the discovery of the world and its many cultures, leading me to gain a better sense of who I am, of my values and my aspirations.

When You're Feeling Lost, Ask for Direction

My search for my first job in America as well as my search for sustainable child care arrangements were two important life challenges that added to my growing faith in the human spirit and divine intervention.

An immigrant trying to land a job in America for the first time is like finding a needle in a haystack. Other than the small circle of family or friends who may have preceded you and are presently giving you free food and shelter, you don't know anyone, and no one knows you. Every credential that you've worked so hard to achieve has become irrelevant because no one has the context of your context. Put simply, your story does not resonate at a level that connects with another person.

When you try to explain that you grew up on a small island in the Philippines, you are not sure what images this conjures in your listener. Although you know your island was very progressive with electricity and water running through all the homes, your listener may be imagining primitive huts. You never really know, because your listener nods politely and says, "Uh, huh, interesting." You try to explain that you studied from the same textbooks used in the American education system. And again, the person you're speaking with nods politely, clearly trying hard to relate.

— —

No one has the context of your context.

— —

The break you might get—if you're lucky—comes from someone who takes one look at you, listens to what you have to say, and takes a chance on you.

This was the predicament I faced when I immigrated to America. I had landed in JFK with a newly minted green card feeling very adventurous. My sisters who had immigrated to the US several years before me settled in Bergen County, New Jersey, and were conveniently living within a block of each other. I was warmly welcomed to stay in my oldest sister's guest room. Two weeks hence, after catching up on jet lag, the time had come for me to find a job. New York City—the Big Apple, the city of opportunities—was a half-hour commute from their house, and so it made sense for me to embark on my job search there. Added to the complexity of looking for a job in New York City was my own history of looking for jobs; I hadn't *really* looked for a job. I landed my previous jobs in the Philippines through connections.

The only way I knew how to find a job was through the *New York Times* "Help Wanted" ads. I'd never seen a newspaper so thick and rich, but that was (and still is) the Sunday *New York Times*. It had a full "Help Wanted" section then, teeming with employment opportunities, organized by type of profession. I eagerly looked for "Accountants" and encircled every possible job that seemed to fit my level of experience.

Then, on Monday morning, I got up early and dressed up to prepare for an interview with a briefcase full of resumes and a purse full of dimes in tow. I took the New Jersey Transit bus right in front of my sister's house to the New York Port Authority terminal. There, I'd select a quiet public phone booth, take out my encircled copy of the *Times* and my purse full of dimes, and start calling. The idea was that when the person on the other line asked when I could come for an interview, I could say I was already at Port Authority and could be in their office right away.

I made up the script in real time: "Good morning, I am calling about your ad in yesterday's New York Times for an accountant...yes, I have a college degree, and a CPA from the Philippines. No, I'm not sure if it counts here. Yes, I have two years' work experience as a financial analyst in the Philippines. No, I don't have any experience working in the States. Yes, I have a green card." I remember I had trouble following the fast English talk of the person on the other line. My sisters advised me to say, "Excuse me?" when I couldn't follow instead of "What?" which would have been perfectly normal to use in the Philippines.

I had never ridden the New York subway system alone, and the subway system was completely unfamiliar, complex, and overwhelming. It was easy to start feeling lost, and I quickly learned to ask for direction. I'd ask the toll booth person while buying my tokens: "I'm going to 123 Broadway, is this the correct train to take?" I got lost a few times. When the train came out of the tunnels on to the street level, this meant that it had just left Manhattan and was on its way to another borough. This was my cue to get off at the next stop and take the train on the opposite track and find my way back.

I must have been at the right phone booth at the right time, because during that first week, one of the calls I made was to an "agent" (now called "recruiter"), who then sent me to the American Express headquarters on Broad Street. I went through a series of interviews, first with the HR Manager and then with the Accounting Manager who would become my boss. I was offered a job as a Senior Accountant on the spot. The HR Manager clarified that although I could start working that Monday, my continued employment was conditional on proper reference checks, even if they were in the Philippines. I quickly obliged and gave them contact information for my previous bosses there. In those days, the letters went via postal mail. It must have taken at least three weeks for the reference checks to be completed. In the meantime, I had started working, and eagerly hoped that my employment would continue.

This is how I landed my first job in America at one of the most respected businesses in the world.

Many years later, those responsible for taking a chance on me–the Accounting Manager and the HR Manager–became my friends and I asked them what made them hire me. They said they actually believed my credentials even if they did not understand the context.

But beyond that, what sold it for them was my refreshing eagerness and honesty about starting to work and building a new life. They saw in this young immigrant a strong belief that she *can* do this. This strong belief in herself and her future seemed deserving of a chance–at least a chance.

I tell this story to those who come to me for advice on job searches. Whatever our circumstances are, the person who hires us is taking a chance on us. They may or may not understand the context of our circumstances because they come from a completely different background, but we need to tell our story anyway–in an honest and vulnerable way–because our story *is* important. In many ways, telling it no matter how different our story may seem, is a way of saying we believe in ourselves. We believe that we deserve a chance. And when the person on the other side sees this, we *will* get that chance.

———

We need to tell our story because our story is important.
It is a way of saying we believe in ourselves and deserve a chance.

———

Years later, I had to overcome another major life challenge. I was once again feeling lost, asked for direction, and once again gained confidence and faith in the human spirit. This time, I also learned to believe that some of the most important people in your life emerge from the most unexpected circumstances, and, with the help of God, you find each other.

I was pregnant with our second child and wondering where and how I'd find a sustainable child care arrangement. Every young working couple in America struggles over finding trustworthy, affordable child care. Being able to afford it is one significant hurdle; finding someone you *will* trust sometimes comes down to a leap of faith.

Actually, we struggled over deciding to have a second child because of the uncertainty of finding trustworthy, reliable and affordable child care. But then, we imagined looking back twenty years hence and saying that the reason we did not have a second child was because we couldn't figure out how to take care of them. No, that would bring a boatload of regrets. We decided to get pregnant with our second child and convinced ourselves that we'd be able to figure this out.

We had managed to cobble up child care for our first child through my husband's aunts, but that was no longer an option. An obvious alternative would have been taking our babies to child care facilities, but we thought this would have been near to impossible for us to sustain. We lived in New Jersey and we both worked in New York. The commute alone was an hour and a half each way, and we couldn't imagine making it on time to pick our babies up before the facility closed. We also couldn't think of taking our babies to commute with us to be dropped off at a New York facility. One of us quitting our job was another obvious option, but neither of us was prepared to make this choice.

We knew that we needed to find a loving adult to provide a consistent presence for our older child and our new baby, making sure they were fed, bathed and cared for no matter how late either or both of us got home. Being immigrants from the Philippines, we also felt it was important for us to find someone who understood our culture, our language, and our food, and shared this with our kids.

What happened next was, I believe to this day, providential.

Here's how I saw divine providence in play: During my pregnancy, I visited the Philippines and reconnected with my first-grade teacher, a nun, Sister Araceli. I can still see her cherubic happy face. This woman did not know the meaning of sadness—she was always cheerful and joyful. During our visit, she asked me the favor of supporting the education of one of her students, a member of our local indigenous tribe. Half-jokingly, I suggested a deal. I would happily do so if she used her heavenly connections to help me find a good person to take care of my kids and household. The deal was sealed.

I returned to the US and without thinking about my request to Sister Araceli, went about searching for a child care provider. Completely out of my comfort zone, I ran an ad in the "Help Wanted" section of the Filipino Reporter. Clearly a non-strategic approach, and for all intents and purposes, a desperate crapshoot of a move. By now, our second child, our son, had been born and was almost three months old. My mother, who flew in from the Philippines to assist temporarily, was eager to return home. Meanwhile, I was about to return to work, and time was running out.

We got one response from the ad. We invited her to interview, and she arrived accompanied by her niece. What I remember the most was her confident, respectful, and calm demeanor. When my parents came into the room to say hello, Clarita stood up in a gesture of respect–a gesture that landed her the job. I knew in my heart that she had integrity, and I could entrust to her the care of my young children.

—

Some of the most important people in your life emerge from the most unexpected circumstances.

—

I believed deeply that she was God's answer to Sister Araceli's prayers for me. Otherwise how could we have found each other? In a leap of faith, I hired her on the spot, without checking references. As it turns out, she was also very qualified, having lived and worked as a housekeeper with Filipino diplomats on foreign assignments.

I asked her how she'd prefer to be called. She was 56 then. Because I was over twenty years younger than her, I did not feel right calling her by her first name, and I felt our young children should address her with deference. She said her nieces and nephews called her "Iyay," which translates to "Auntie" in her dialect. And that's how it came to be that I, my husband, our two children, and everyone who visited our home, including my parents, came to call her Iyay.

Iyay proved to be the consummate surrogate mother, trustworthy companion, and loyal friend. She was an excellent cook, amazing housekeeper, and talented seamstress. She cared for our children deeply and lovingly. She shared with them the hard life lessons she learned, and how she managed to navigate her way to better conditions.

The woman who helped us raise and nurture our kids and keep order in our home had a hard life. Her parents died while she was very young, leaving her care to her oldest sister. They were poor, so she had to stop going to school when she was in third grade to help support the family. She initially lived with local families as a housekeeper, then one of these families referred her to a family friend living in the city of Manila, and that's how she got to the city. There, she learned how to sew, a talent she discovered she had. (Years later, we would be the beneficiary of this talent as she created beautiful Halloween costumes for our children and sewed amazing window treatments for our house.) She met a man and married him, while she continued to work as a housekeeper and a seamstress. She'd say that the man she married turned out to be a drunk, and she left him when she caught him trying to steal and sell her sewing machine. A resourceful and confident woman, Iyay found her way to employment with a family in the diplomatic corps who took her with them in their foreign posts. She was coming out of this employment and visiting her niece in New Jersey when I ran my ad and she decided to apply.

Iyay stayed with us for eleven years. She was not the easiest person to live with. A strong woman with a strong opinion, we differed in how we wanted to run the household. I found myself deferring to her, realizing that the truth was, she *was* running my household. On the other hand, she was deferential to me on how to raise the kids, and faithfully implemented the rules set for them to follow in the house. In many ways, Iyay and I found our way around each other, respecting the unspoken boundaries we set for each other's role.

I sponsored her to become a US permanent resident, which enabled her to become a US citizen. When she finally received her green card, I encouraged her to retire and rest. Iyay is now 86 years old and still very much a part of our lives. She nursed me to wellness, washing my hair when I had cancer. She visited to help our son pack for college, cooking his favorite meals. She traveled the distance to visit my mother, then afflicted with Alzheimer's. She is a constant source of laughter for our daughter, who dutifully checks in with her by phone. She was a special guest at our son's wedding, where she proudly spoke about how she started caring for him as an infant. Ever confident and self-assured, she has no problem arguing with a train conductor about getting her senior citizen discount, and she still visits her extended family in the Philippines once a year.

Little did I know when I was looking for a live-in child care provider that in Iyay we would find so much more–a loving aunt, a caring nurse, and a loyal friend. She was an angel sent to me in my hour of need and continues to be a source of inspiration for all of us, particularly for our children. She is a model of hard work, resilience, and generosity. It was a leap of faith–hiring Iyay on the spot. And sometimes, that's all we need to do.

I have come to believe that I found my first job in America and the woman who helped raise our kids, because I was feeling lost and asked for direction. Then, with the help of good people in the world and God, I found my way.

Believe That You Can

Finding my way and learning along the way defined my life from my 30s to my 60s. As a reluctant accountant who really wanted to be a psychologist or a diplomat, I could not have imagined the serendipitous turns my career took, and the moves my family and I had to make. I have been asked many times how this all happened.

The truth is I did not plan it this way. I've come to realize that unconsciously I had the curiosity and audacity to believe in my capacity to meet *any* challenge that came my way, and this attitude opened up possibilities for me.

I had a thriving career at American Express, having been promoted several times. I had just finished my MBA, had a six-month-old baby and was commuting an hour and a half each way when I discovered my need for "balance." I don't think I actually put a name to what I was missing–after all, I thought I was doing everything I wanted to do. Despite having a loving and supportive husband, I felt completely overwhelmed and uncentered. If one small thing fell off my schedule–the train ran late, for example–it felt as if my world would fall apart. I was trying to construct this perfect world wherein there was no place for imperfection and started realizing that this was not possible.

While my choices were limited, it became clear to me that what I needed more of was time. Time to be with my family, time to simply be.

Through a recruiter, I found a job as Director of Finance at a small tech start-up in New Jersey. It was a tough choice–giving up a promising career at American Express, but with this move, I gained at least three hours daily from not having to commute.

By the end of the first week, I knew for sure that I'd made the wrong move. American Express was the epitome of Corporate America. Not only did I suddenly miss the luxurious office environment, I missed the camaraderie of the amazing professionals with whom I worked. I found myself in a one-floor office in downtown Hackensack, NJ. While my new colleagues were nice, I felt in my gut that I did not belong there. Every time I walked into work, I knew I had to get out. The only thing that helped me keep my bearings was that I was now closer to home.

I started looking for another job, responding to an ad in the newspaper that led me to an interview with Kwasha Lipton (KL), a prestigious benefits consulting firm. I was completely honest in my interviews: I said I was looking to find balance in my life and this is why I left American Express, but the company I moved to was not what I thought it was. Maybe I was being too honest and vulnerable in the interview, but to my happy surprise, KL turned out to be one of the rare progressive companies in 1986 that believed in and supported work/life balance. The company policy enabled all employees–male or female–with pre-school children to spend more time at home. The work arrangements included telecommuting, flex-time, and other creative ways of working remotely. I could not believe that such a company existed, and I could not believe that they offered me a job as Director of Accounting.

I was looking for balance in my work and life.

I accepted and discovered that KL was one of the jewels of the industry–a very successful professional partnership with expertise in employee benefits design and administration. The partners' perks were shared with all the employees. They had free coffee and soda. A free gym, with trainers on staff, t-shirts and towels at your disposal. A car wash in the basement. Grand summer and holiday parties. Fresh flowers every day. It was truly a special place. I thrived, rising to the position of Principal, with full responsibility for finance, treasury and accounting.

The aspiration to "have it all" meant making choices. During my time at KL, my husband and I had our second child and moved to our second home. My choice to leave American Express allowed me to find the time I needed to be with my growing family. I was able to take and pick up the kids from school, discovering that conversations in the car could offer the best opportunity to discuss important lessons in life. For the next ten years I stayed at KL, enjoying and sustaining my work/life balance. There was absolutely no reason to leave.

—

Having it all meant making choices.

—

But then I was seduced. A clever recruiter found me and spoke of an amazing opportunity: a leadership role in the transformation of Bellcore (the baby bells' Bell Labs) to a commercial operation, and its potential IPO. The role was divisional CFO of Bellcore's $300M consulting business unit, with the promise of better pay, stock options, and a bright future. It would require moving 50 miles from Bergen County to Monmouth County, but they would relocate my family–literally buy our house outright and move us. How could I say no?

I said yes, and we moved. The next five years were grueling. I didn't know what I didn't know. I didn't know how difficult it was to move an entire family–no matter that it was only 50 miles away. My husband still worked in New York City, and while our new home was closer to work than it ever was, the responsibility of getting the kids resettled into their new schools was far more complicated than I imagined it to be. We missed our family and all our old friends. Transforming this company was not easy. My boss who hired me got fired within six months of my move. It became clear that the company was not ready for an IPO. We switched direction to a strategic sale.

I didn't know what I didn't know.

Work was tough but I learned a lot. I learned how to teach brilliant engineers the rudiments of a P&L. I participated in "road shows" and learned what it took to make a pitch to potential investors. I learned how to monetize intellectual property, leading mergers and acquisitions deals later on.

I also learned how important my family was to me, and how—no matter what—their safety, happiness, and well-being are what make me keep going. As the kids both became active with numerous school activities, my husband and I consciously and meticulously planned our schedules to ensure that we both shared not only in the responsibility but also in being with each of the children to experience with them their ups and downs. Of course, there were mishaps. I was running late to catch my son's first school play and didn't realize I was speeding. A young cop pulled me over, and as he was writing up my ticket, I gave him a lecture on how he could be a better public servant by developing empathy for working mothers. Another time, one of the non-working mothers in our carpool threatened to cancel our arrangements if I continued to be late picking up her son. The time I saw the two boys waiting for me with the school custodian because the school had closed and I was the last mother to come for pick-up was, admittedly, bad parenting.

As I got busier in my work, I actually became more adept in the balancing act. Once, I accompanied our daughter to a national junior tennis competition while I was running an important acquisition deal. I thought I had perfectly scheduled the multi-time-zone conference call around the time she would have finished her match. What I didn't anticipate was a much longer match, with her "splitting" sets with her opponent. Luckily, I had deputized one of our lawyers to start the call, so there was no harm done. I joined the call and closed the deal, though I'm sure everyone was wondering where that ping-pong sound of balls was coming from.

Through all the busyness of my work at Bellcore, we managed most of the time to have dinner together, share the day's stories, and be a family. I don't know how we did it, but we did.

Then, as if all of a sudden, Bellcore got sold, the telecom bubble burst, and I was out of a job.

I took that summer off. In the midst of those five years, my beloved nephew Vincent died, and his death caused me to reconsider what my work was. What is my work about in the real sense of work/life balance—a tenet I've learned to value so much? For the first time in my life, I thought about how I could find work that truly integrates my life values. And this is when serendipity comes into play.

———

How can I find work that truly integrates my life values?

———

A friend talked me into attending a networking event, where I sat beside a recruiter who asked me what I was doing. I told her I was out of work, but was seriously assessing where I'd work next, having come to the conclusion that I needed to find work that connects with my sense of values. She invited me to apply for the opportunity to run a private school in New York City. The Ethical Culture Fieldston School (ECFS), steeped in the values of ethics, diversity, and sustainability, would undergo a major campus expansion, and was looking for someone to run its operations as well as the campus expansion project.

Why my inexperience at working for a not-for-profit–much less run a pre-K–12 school, and never mind a serious construction project–did not get in the way of my applying and getting offered the position is, in retrospect, probably due to the combined effect of my audacious belief that "I can" and good old luck. Truth be told, at the same time I got offered this position, I turned down a lucrative job offer as a telecom VP with big money/options job because my would-be boss told me she was hardly able to join her family for dinner once a week.

I felt eager to discover what it was to work in an environment where my core values could be aligned with the organization's values.

This is how I left the corporate world and joined the mission-driven world of not-for-profits. I went back to commuting to New York City. The kids were sixteen and thirteen by now, and I felt more comfortable spending less time at home.

People ask me how I managed the shift from corporate to not-for-profit, and I'm not sure how to answer that. There are structural differences–governance being the big one–but otherwise, it's basically the same. Fundamentally, it is about people working together.

We got so much done in the time I was at ECFS, and again, I learned so much. We completed the campus expansion project on time and on budget. I learned how to negotiate with unions. I figured out how to work with faculty. I even taught a class or two. Most importantly, I learned about the great values of ethics, diversity, and sustainability. The school believed in them, instilled them in their students, and the staff lived by them. More than ever, I knew how important my family was to me, and how they continued to motivate and inspire me to do what I could to make a difference in the world. I survived a bout with cancer during this time, and this experience strengthened my resolve to continue to find work that would create a positive impact in the world.

While I had no intention of leaving ECFS, I knew I had begun to feel restless. Our kids had by now gone off to college, and the feeling of an empty nest was nagging at me. I had also bought in to the concept of creating a sustainable life, and I felt the life that my husband and I were living at this point was less than sustainable.

I was back to commuting, spending three hours daily on the road. We had a big house in New Jersey that required substantial maintenance, not to mention hefty taxes. There must be a better way to live somewhere else, I kept telling my husband. He said, "Where?"

Enter recruiter number five. I think this is when I eerily started to believe the notion that "when I declare something to the universe, it responds." The recruiter found me somehow, and spoke of a place called Charlottesville, Virginia, where the University of Virginia is located. There was an opportunity for the role of Senior Associate Dean for Finance and Administration for the Darden Business School. I researched Charlottesville. It was ranked as one of the top places to live in the US. I looked up Darden. One of the top 20.

—

When I declare something to the "universe," it responds.

—

So here I was again, having never worked in higher education, being considered for–and believing–that I can do this job. I convinced my husband to check it out. We went. We liked it. I was offered the job. I accepted. We moved. Not without pain. Fall 2008 happened, and we found ourselves having to sell our beloved house in a down market. The seven months it took for our house to be sold while I was already working in Charlottesville were difficult for me and my husband. He also retired from his job of 25 years and moved to a place where he didn't know anybody. We adjusted, made new friends, and he eventually started working again. His reinvention is in itself an inspiring story.

Having worked and lived in New York/New Jersey all our lives in the States, the meaning of living in the south became evident. I learned how to navigate my way in a large university, becoming sensitized to how things were done in the north versus the south. We got used to it and learned to love Charlottesville. I once again thrived. I not only ran the place well, I also learned to teach, and to do that well. By now, it was clear to me that I was an effective leader, and thanks to a beloved colleague, we created and taught a course on Global Leadership. It was a hit, landing in the top ten percentile of the students' approval ratings. I became intrigued by executive coaching, a service that we used for our MBA students. I signed up and got myself certified as an executive coach.

I did not realize that trouble was brewing. Trouble for me. An institutional-wide assessment I initiated to create a more effective organization led to the elimination of my position. I suppose I had a feeling that my boss did not like me anymore, but never did I think that he would actually force me out. Well, he did. I was heartbroken. I felt completely betrayed. This experience is by far my most humbling experience. While the record will show that my position was eliminated, I felt I was actually fired.

I went away with my dog for three days, to an Airbnb cottage facing the Chesapeake Bay. We walked, I cried. I wrote, I cried. Then I stopped crying and decided I would launch my own coaching and consulting practice. I would call it "The Next Step." Because this is what I do; I take the next step.

This is what I do: I take the next step.

For the next year and a half, I went solo, sharing an office suite with a chiropractor and an acupuncturist, both women. We used to joke that a visit to our office can fix anything. I found my first client, a former colleague, while I was shopping for my "client's chair" at a consignment shop in town. On my first day in my office, at about 3:30 p.m., I called my husband to tell him I was going home. He said, "Sure, but why are you calling me?" I said, "Because I'm not yet used to leaving my work without telling anyone else."

I discovered my love for coaching. I found it extremely rewarding to help a client open up to new possibilities, enabling forward motion. I learned so much from my practice. I learned to listen more actively, without judgment. I learned to empathize. I learned not to direct, but to simply help my clients discover on their own. I felt good about what I was doing. *But* I missed the hustle and bustle of working in a group, of leading an organization. I missed the work of motivating and running teams to get things done.

And here's the proof of concept for "ask, and the universe responds"—a call from recruiter number six. "Are you in the market?" My response: "For what?" Their response: "The COO role at the Museum of Contemporary Art in Chicago." Our son went to school in Chicago and was still living there, so the initial appeal was the opportunity to visit him. I thought the recruiter was being very clever, inviting me to apply to make the pool of candidates more interesting. After all, I am a diversity candidate, have a relatively interesting background, and why not? Aside from the appeal of my son's proximity, the position sounded very cool. So, I threw my name into the hat, with some expectation that I would be out of the running by round two or three.

I must have, once again, projected an unshakeable confidence in my belief that "I can" because without any museum experience and no clue about contemporary art, I was offered the position. The responsibilities also included leading the museum's major space renovation.

Considering a "commuting marriage" was never on the table, but my husband was loving his work, raising money for medical research, and clearly did not want to give up his job. Someone once advised me to check in on how you feel about something before you jump in. I checked in. I felt really, really excited. I was completely intrigued by the opportunity, and after a thorough deliberation with my trusted council–my husband and my kids–I accepted and moved to Chicago. We embarked on a commuting marriage, and we have made it work. Short direct flights and technology were invaluable; we FaceTimed every day and visited every ten days or so.

Time, like space, gets quickly filled when it's open. The trick is to protect it, tuck it away, and savor it. I now have one hour of "Terry time" scheduled in my daily calendar. Whether that hour is consumed by pressing work or walking around the block is a choice I make. The busyness of life can be overwhelming, and I've learned that making time for me and for those I care for creates the balance I need to become a better leader, a better parent, and a better person. Undoubtedly, time with my family is an important cornerstone that fuels my success at work.

I've come to call this building a sustainable lifestyle. A lifestyle where one can find purpose, good health, and growth. Finding balance does not apply only to those with family responsibilities. I have coaching clients with no such obligations who come to understand that this balance is what they are missing too. It could very well be a passion not explored, a community contribution dreamed of, a connection yearned for–all set aside because it's been "too busy." I've learned to screen for my most important life decisions with the question: Will this decision lead to a life that will sustain me, a life that will help me stay healthy, be impactful, and still enable me to continue to learn and grow? It is a mantra that I practice and preach.

——

Balance creates a sustainable life.

——

As the COO of one of the most respected contemporary art museums in the world, I was often asked, "So tell me about contemporary art." I'd generally smile before saying, "I really don't know much about contemporary art, but I'm learning." I wasn't being modest; that was the truth.

Three years later, the museum's major renovation project was completed–on time and on budget and lauded by critics as 2017's best renovation in Chicago. I learned to love Chicago. I became closer to our son, and his girlfriend then, his wife now. My husband and I not only adjusted to a commuting marriage; we learned to do it well. Our family is tighter than ever before. I learned to work with the most amazing creative talents, whom I call my colleagues and friends. I figured out how to sustain my coaching practice. I became part of an organization that is making a difference in the world by creating a safe space for our society to engage in conversations about relevant issues of our times through art–where thousands of Chicago public school children, teens and families gather and learn.

I continue to believe that I am here, on this earth, for a purpose. And while there is life, I will continue to be open and attentive to the possibilities of what and how that purpose is evolving. I continue to believe that I will be steered in the direction that will help me continue to serve this purpose. I continue to believe that whatever opportunity or challenge arrives, I will be ready, and I will be able to meet it wholeheartedly. Until then, I strive to be better. A better boss and colleague, a better coach and teacher, a better wife, mother, sister and friend–just a better person. I believe that I can.

Live Within Your Means

Money seems to be one of those mysteries in life, and the sheer idea that it needs to be dealt with can send shivers of fear into some of the smartest, most creative, and most confident people I know. They'd simply say, "I don't think I can." Money can have such a painful and strong hold on anyone who is not clear about their relationship with money. In my work as a life coach, I have come across many clients who find themselves at a standstill when it comes to making important life decisions because of their fear of money–having too little, or in some cases, having too much. It is a predicament that is shared by the poor and the rich alike.

As I have come to truly embrace the belief that balance creates a sustainable life, the essence of money and the role that it plays in one's life has become much more relevant and profound to me. I've become an advocate for financial literacy: having the know-how to make informed and effective decisions about one's financial resources. Understanding what money means to you, learning how to live within your means, and ultimately figuring out how to use money as a means to the end is key to living a rewarding, fulfilling and sustainable life.

While my financial training helped, I got my money sense early on from my parents. I grew up with parents who couldn't have had more divergent attitudes towards money.

My mother's parents were poor, and while her father was employed, he earned only enough to buy the basic necessities of life. She'd say that their small house was in such disrepair that when it rained, they needed to sleep in another part of the house to avoid getting wet from the leaky roof her parents could not afford to fix. Still, her mother saw to it that they lived "well." We now marvel at the beautiful plates that my maternal grandmother somehow accumulated, as well as the lovely slippers, and delicate hand-woven silk scarves. She had classy taste and she passed this on to my mother.

My mother and her brother found their way out of poverty by educating themselves. They were both very smart, graduated at the top of their class, and earned merit scholarships to go to college. Even then, when they went to college, they felt the painful isolation that poverty brings. My mother worked as a professor's assistant to pay for her school supplies and told us, her children, how she'd salvage scraps of paper to use for taking class notes. She did not have any money for party clothes and was very grateful to receive hand-me-downs from the professor she worked for. Similarly, her brother would write papers for his classmates, or complete their homework in exchange for their slightly worn shoes. They continued to be stellar students and finished at the top of their college graduating classes.

My father's mother was a woman ahead of her time. She was what we would call now a serial entrepreneur.

She was a pioneer, an innovator who created business-es that had not existed before. A merchandiser, she built her wealth initially by buying and selling livestock, then seized opportunities to accumulate agricultural and commercial real estate. The story goes that by the time my father was a young boy, my paternal grandmother was so busy that my father had to be brought to wherever she was, so they could have a meal together. We can speculate that she compensated for her absence by giving in to my father's every wish, including and especially access to money. He'd recollect with a chuckle how, as a teenager, he'd simply open his mother's money drawer and slide out a stash of bills, no questions asked. Neither son nor mother knew how much he took on any given day. His childhood was full of mischief, missed days at school, suspensions, and, later on, drinking and gambling.

While they were from the same town, my parents did not move in the same social circle, and somehow met just as World War II was ending, fell in love, and got married. The two of them could not have been more different in upbringing and values—particularly when it came to money.

Realizing that her son had never worked a day in his life and did not know how to make a living, my paternal grandmother took on the responsibility of supporting my parents. She invested in a pharmacy for my mother so she could have her own means, stay home, and raise the anticipated children. Whatever other money she needed (the pharmacy did not make any money)—all she needed to do was ask—either my father or my grandmother.

Despite this invitation to an open expense account, my mother decided to return to work when I, the youngest child, was about three years old. She'd later explain to me and my siblings that she went back to work as a college instructor because she didn't want to ask for money from anybody anymore. She wanted to be able to spend–buy her kids' shoes for example–and be able to do it on her own.

A paradox of a man, my father continued to squander his money gambling, while also being very generous to communities and families in need of help. He inherited landholdings from his mother and donated some of the land for schools, churches, and community centers. His generosity made a long-lasting difference in many people's lives. Still, his gambling wins and losses were so legendary in our small town that I remember hearing about some of them from my classmates. "Oh, I heard your father lost a few hundred thousand pesos this weekend." I'd awkwardly say that I didn't know.

—

My mother went back to work because she didn't want to have to ask anyone for money.

—

My mother saved whatever she could. She taught us, her children, how to save and opened savings accounts for each of us. Each of us had little passport size booklets that showed how much money we had in the bank. She was proud of what she was able to save. Let me be clear: She was not a penny-pincher. Because my father's sources of income were also hers, she was able to afford her classy style and she made sure that she and her entire family–we, her children as well as my father, were always dressed nicely. Like her mother, she invested in some beautiful jewelry pieces that my sisters and I now proudly call our own heirlooms.

This is all the backdrop to how I started to learn the meaning and value of money and its impact on someone's life. I learned from observing my parents. My father spent and enjoyed his money, and while we can all judge that he wasted it, I know he found joy in spending it. He was also very generous, using his money to make a difference in the lives of others. My mother had a very measured approach to money, and I wonder if she could have been more generous to herself and to others.

—

My father's generosity made a lasting difference in many people's lives.

—

I continued to save throughout my life. I'm still saving. I have taught our kids to save. My mother used to say, if you have 100 pesos, just put away 10 pesos. Even today's financial gurus would agree, maintaining that a 10-percent savings off your income is a basic step to financial health. I also don't gamble and would choose to invest in the more economical (vs. luxurious) version of a car or a house. I spend on memorable experiences that I feel enrich our lives.

One of the things we associate with our financial means is our ability to make a difference. We feel stymied from doing anything because we are not sure if we can afford to do so. This became evident recently during a dinner hosted by a friend among some ten like-minded women professionals, coincidentally in the aftermath of the Charlottesville racial violence in August 2017. Our conversation naturally turned to the question: What can each of us do to make a difference? The range of possibilities became overwhelming, and we found ourselves back at the fundamental question: Where do we begin?

We were stumped. This group of highly successful, intelligent, and capable professional women seemed paralyzed at the enormity of the challenge we were facing. How could we begin to change what seemed to be a new course in the history of our great country?

I'm not sure what prompted me, but I said, "We can each start with small acts, because small acts matter." I shared the stories of three small acts. All were opportunities I stumbled upon, and I simply decided to take the next step to move forward.

—

Small acts matter.

—

During my stint as a board member at Virginia's community college, I started what I called "the first American fund," a needs-based scholarship fund for immigrants or first-generation Americans. I was one, and I have benefited from the graciousness and generosity of the American people. I felt this was one way of giving back and keeping true to the ideals that America has been built upon and that made it great. A democracy where everyone, regardless of race or origin of birth, has an equal right to life, liberty and the pursuit of happiness. I have replicated this at the MCA, funding a paid internship for a college student, because I learned to believe that enabling this kind of access will create a virtuous cycle of building future leadership talent.

—

Enabling access will create a virtuous cycle of building future talent.

—

I also spoke about teaching in Virginia's prison for women. Our class discussions gave the women in my class the opportunity to reflect on the leaders they admire, and the traits they can emulate from these leaders. We also explored the businesses they'd start when they get out of prison: a beauty salon; a safe house for recovering addicts; a bakery; and since they couldn't get a driver's license, a transportation service to ferry ex-convicts to/from their place of work The possibility of emulating an admired leader's traits and starting their own business had not previously dawned upon my students. Our lessons empowered them to imagine these possibilities.

I shared how I am supporting a young student's high-school education in the Philippines. She writes me and shares her grades regularly and it is very rewarding to witness a young woman dream of her future that will not be bound by the circumstances of poverty and lack of access to which she was born.

I shared how all this didn't take much. In the context of big and small acts, these acts are relatively small. While I am very grateful that I can afford to provide this financial support, doing so did not require wealth.

A week following our dinner party, I received a note from our hostess, who said that "small acts matter" resonated so much with her, that she wrote to some close friends asking for donations to help fund a program for Chicago public school children. She said that within a week, she raised over $6,000–money that will fund books for 200 students.

To make a difference in the world, we don't have to be rich. We can begin with small acts, because small acts matter.

In my advocacy for financial literacy, I've developed a workshop, building my teaching material around the acronym MONEY. M is to understand what money Means to you, helping you understand your relationship with money. O is to get a good sense of what you Own and what you Owe–your net worth. N is to understand your Needs as opposed to your wants. E is to be clear on what you are Earning and your capacity to earn more. Y is to understand how you can build wealth and use your money for what you Yearn for.

When I taught at Virginia's prison for women, I learned even more about how becoming financially literate was of paramount importance. One young lady had been incarcerated for over ten years for bouncing checks. And while the state provided them with their basic needs: a set of uniforms, a bar of soap and a roll of toilet paper, they also need to reckon with the economic system in place within the prison system. They need to purchase their other necessities–feminine hygiene supplies for example–from the wages they earn, which at that time was twenty-five cents an hour.

At the end of our term together, I tasked my students with developing a business plan for the business they have dreamt of launching when they get out of prison. One of my constant sources of inspiration is a note from one of my students. It reads, *"I just wanted to take a moment to thank you for reaching out to the ladies of this correction center. The knowledge that you have taken the time to share with us is more valuable than you could possibly know. You have helped me to realize that my dreams can become my reality. Thank you so much for your time, attention and compassion..."*

I hope to continue to share money sense with those who may not have it yet. It is key to living a sustainable and rewarding life. Living within our means is where we all have to start.

Healing Takes Time and Care

No matter how much you believe you can handle anything, life throws at you the proverbial "curve balls" that rock your world and shake your faith. For me, this came in the sudden and tragic loss of young loved ones, 9/11, and a bout with cancer.

Grief is deeply personal, and each of us deals with it the way we know how. Except we don't know how. It strikes us and takes a foothold that cannot be shaken, that we don't necessarily want to shake. We hold on to the fragments of what could have been, only to be left with what was. What is will never be the same. We keep running in our heads what we could have done to change the outcome, to prevent the tragedy, but it is done, and if there's one thing that's final, it's death. The loss can be so profound, paralyzing us to our core. So how to move forward?

I've had my share of grief, and three losses stand out as deep and life-changing. From them, I've learned that we can only move forward if we embrace and honor our loss.

One of my family's deepest losses preceded me but will affect me for the rest of my life. As a child growing up living with my maternal grandparents, one of my unforgettable memories is Tio Pepe's framed life-size picture depicting a handsome young man in full military gear. He was my mother's older brother. Legend has it that as a young officer of the joint US/Philippine Air Force during World War II, he had so much daring that he single-handedly engaged in aerial dogfights against the Japanese pilots. For this he earned the US Distinguished Service Cross.

During the Japanese occupation of the Philippines, Tio Pepe and a buddy decided to make a raft to sail to Australia to meet up with General Douglas McArthur's forces. They got lost at sea and were never found. We know this to be true because there was a witness, another friend of theirs who didn't swim well and saw them sail off. One of my dearest treasures is Tio Pepe's note to his family while he was in hiding, a note my mother entrusted to me.

In beautiful penmanship, he wrote, "Right now, we are a part of God's children that ceaselessly roam because they can't stay in one place. There are still a lot of good people left on the earth, however, who wholeheartedly offer shelter to these wanderers. So what have we to fear?"

Tio Pepe was awarded many military distinctions. Several military stations in the Philippines were named after him and commemorative stamps were issued in his honor. Still, I could not imagine how his disappearance broke his parents' and his sister's hearts. My mother, his sister, would tell us stories about how their mother, my grandmother, would wail in grief, unexpectedly and uncontrollably. I believe my grandmother died more than forty years later still waiting for Tio Pepe to show up at her doorstep.

Decades later, during one of our summer holidays in the Philippines my mother accompanied me, my husband and young children to vacation in Boracay, the island of Aklan. My mother and I found ourselves alone in a rented boat while the rest of our company went snorkeling. All of a sudden, my mother exclaimed, "I think we are on the waters where your Tio Pepe disappeared."

As if on cue, a huge beautiful butterfly fluttered right by our faces. My mother got more excited, "That is a sign from your Tio Pepe," she said. "Mom, please, don't be so superstitious; it's just a butterfly," I said. My mother, the scientist, was indignant. "Terry, do you see how far we are from land? A butterfly cannot navigate that distance," she matter-of-factly declared.

Right there and then, she declared that she'd have a tombstone built for Tio Pepe, a final resting place that she had neglected to create. And she did. It was my mother's way of honoring her loss and making some sense of the grief that has gripped her for over fifty years.

Tio Pepe would have been 100 years old in April 2018, and our dream of honoring him with a bust at his birthplace's town plaza has also become a reality. A fitting honor for a young man a town lost, a hero a country gained, an uncle I never met, who in many ways, changed the course of my life forever. To think he was only 26 years old when he left us.

—

"Right now, we are a part of God's children that ceaselessly roam because they can't stay in one place. There are still a lot of good people left on the earth who wholeheartedly offer shelter to these wanderers. So what have we to fear?"

—

Vincent, my nephew and middle sister's son also left us when he was barely 26 years old. The difference of course is we knew Vincent. The first Filipino American to be born to our family this side of the world, he was named after my father, Vicente. Vincent quickly became the apple of everyone's eye. Smart, funny, kind and humble, he easily became the life of our family gatherings.

Vincent became my young children's "chief cousin" and they simply loved and adored him. I think it's because they knew he loved and adored them. He showed them, he told them, and he always went out of his way to let them know it. He walked from school to play with them. He tickled them to tears. He organized annual trips to New Jersey's Great Adventure Park and inspired them to collect Coke cans to help defray the cost of the entrance fee. He was generous, kind, and loving to all of us, his family. He was as smart as he was humble, with a sharp wit, the kind that in my humble opinion, can cut through any barriers.

Life got busy. Vincent went off to medical school, I was raising two kids, and we were all making a living. Vincent's graduation from medical school was clearly a major milestone for our immigrant family: the first Filipino-American generation made its mark when its first-born graduated with honors from Tulane University's medical school. Vincent started his residency in surgery and we were all proud.

Two months into his residency, Vincent was found dead in his Brooklyn apartment. He had committed suicide. A couple of days later, my ten-year-old son, Vincent's number one fan, dreamt of Vincent. Vincent had a message to all of us: he was sorry for the grief that he had caused us, but he wanted to let us know that he was in heaven and it's the best anyone could ever imagine. Our son reported that when he asked Vincent if he could come back because we all missed him, Vincent replied that it was against the rules, but he could always come back in our dreams, because that's how they actually do it.

This comforted me then and continues to comfort me. I went to therapy to learn how to cope with our deep loss. I introduced my young kids to therapy. They needed to know the truth and learn how to cope with such a painful truth. My therapist explained to us that not unlike a heart attack, suicide is a brain attack. All systems fail, and the connections get cut off. Therapy helped us cope.

Together, my sister, Vincent's mom, with my older sister and I, found ways to celebrate Vincent and honor his life. They established scholarships in schools that Vincent attended. We started a small family foundation, called "Vincent's Gift" that supports mental health awareness for incoming medical residents.

Recently, a well-intended physician approached us, asking to include Vincent's story in her project about suicide in the medical field. This prompted Vincent's mother and me to speak about our grief, and–21 years later–we feel we have healed. Not one day passes that we don't still miss Vincent, but we have honored our loss, nurtured our grief, and feel at peace.

—

Honor your loss and nurture your grief.

—

While losing Tio Pepe and Vincent were clear tragic losses that we spent time grieving and honoring, I had a personal loss that I feel I completely minimized. My first pregnancy ended in a miscarriage. The life of a working, commuting graduate student was not easy. But I had it all planned: I'd get pregnant during my last semester in grad school, have the baby, and go on maternity leave as soon as I graduated. Almost three years into my MBA program, commuting over an hour each day, I was taking classes two nights a week, and also traveling for business. I had landed on the fast track, and having received a series of promotions, I felt I had become one of the women in the 80s who was going to have it all.

I learned I was pregnant during a business trip to the UK. This happy news brought such joyful anticipation to me, my husband, and our extended families. I was even more energized and continued the hectic pace of work, school, and commuting. I was about 8 weeks pregnant when I started to bleed. My doctor advised me to lie down and rest. I did. The bleeding progressively got worse. I was losing the baby in a miscarriage. Webster's has two definitions of "miscarriage": the spontaneous expulsion of a fetus before it is able to survive independently; and an unsuccessful outcome of something planned. Both were applicable, and I could not do anything about it. I felt completely helpless. My doctor advised me not to worry, it is nature's way, and that I would feel better when I got pregnant again. Still, for 33 years, I felt a deep regret that I had not honored this loss. Finally, on my husband's 66th birthday, we planted a magnolia tree in memory of this young life which flourishes now, not on earth but in the heavenly garden.

In memory of this young life, a tree flourishes now in the heavenly garden.

Despite these sudden and tragic losses, life went on. We became parents to a daughter, then a son. Then, one day, life threw a whopping curve ball that changed the world forever. September 11, 2001 started out as a beautiful, crisp early fall day on the East Coast. I remember noticing that there was not a cloud in the sky. We piled out of the house as we would normally. My husband went off earlier than us because he was commuting from New Jersey to New York, the kids went to school and I drove to a meeting in New Jersey.

As we were starting our meeting, my cell phone rang. It was my husband calling from the train station. Apparently, he noticed a major commotion as he was getting off the PATH train at the World Trade Center (WTC). I recall him saying, "I hear shots or explosions... and everyone is running." I responded, "Then go back on the train and go home." He said, "No, they are all running out," to which I said, "Well, then run out!" He said, "I'll call you later." Then the lines went dead.

Heading back to my meeting, I noticed that everyone had convened in front of a TV screen, staring and speechless. As I joined them, I saw footage of an airplane flying into the World Trade Center. It was around the same time as when my husband called me.

The next hour was a blur. I think everyone who saw this on TV went into shock; and while adrenalin was flowing high to those in the midst of this terror, the rest of us were completely paralyzed, frozen into inaction.

My cell phone rang again. It was my sister reporting that my husband reached her land line and asked that she call me to assure me he was safe. He had walked to his office, which was literally behind the WTC, and they had been asked to stay indoors until "cleared to leave."

Another call came through—my kids! They were at school, and the school administration had gathered all the kids who had a parent working in the WTC area. They were both very upset on the phone. "Why haven't you called us? How is Dad? Where is he?" I don't know why I did not think of calling them or driving home to pick them up. I didn't even think they were aware of this terror raging beyond the safety of their classrooms. After I assured them he was fine, in his office, waiting to be "cleared to leave," I left the meeting that never happened and picked the kids up from school. I don't think we have ever hugged as tightly as we did when we saw each other that day.

For the next two endless hours, we were glued to the TV, in shock, not knowing what to say or do, waiting for my husband's call. The land line finally rang. Apparently, my husband managed to catch a train leaving from Manhattan, scheduled to arrive in New Jersey within the hour. We picked him up from the train station and wondered how many of the cars parked in the train station had owners who were not lucky enough to get out. We were living in the town of Holmdel, NJ, right next to Middletown, NJ, a popular residential hub for Wall Street employees.

My husband was a close eye-witness to many of the stories we heard on TV. Apparently, he managed to catch a train from NJ to land safely at the WTC that morning. We all know now that the building collapsed shortly thereafter, and the commotion he heard and called me about turned out to be the sound of the explosion when the plane hit the building. As he instinctively tried to make his way to his workplace right behind the WTC, he saw up-close, people jumping out of the tower. He got into his workplace just in time before they locked down his building. He saw the WTC collapse and the neighboring area dissolve into a dark pit of horror and ash. When he was cleared to leave, he walked through the debris, and several blocks later heard the familiar sound of a train in the subway. He took this train, landed in Penn Station, where there was a packed train bound for our NJ train station. This all sounds too good to be true. It is too good, and it is true.

One of my son's friends whose father worked at Cantor Fitzgerald asked my son the following day if his dad came home, because his friend's dad didn't.

Tragedy struck, and it changed the world. We are grateful that my husband was spared. It was very close, and a jarring reminder of how fragile life is.

Since then, my husband, kids and I make it a point to say "I love you" at the end of each phone conversation or at the end of each visit. It has been our way of reminding each other that each encounter, no matter how ordinary, is precious time together, not to be taken for granted.

—

Remember to say, "I love you."

—

We got past 9/11, moved on, and in the year that I was turning fifty, my life was in full gear. All was good in my world. I felt invincible. My career was thriving, so was my husband's. Both kids were doing well in school, and we had a comfortable home.

Looking forward to my big 5-0, I booked a dream trip to cruise around the Mediterranean, with my husband and our two kids. My treat. We couldn't wait.

The message on my machine was vague–a request for me to call back for a follow-up appointment. I called back and learned that my mammogram results showed "something" that they were "not sure" about, so a mammogram retake was necessary. Mammogram number two was not clear either, and I went through a couple of progressive biopsies. I was finally told that the results were "negative." I breathed a major sigh of relief and, a couple of weeks later, took our regular spring break to Hilton Head Island.

During this blissful week of walking on the beach, I discovered that my biopsy wound had re-opened, the size of a nickel gaping on my right breast. I went back to my breast surgeon in New Jersey (let's call him Dr. X), who checked the wound, instructed me on how to clean it, and assured me that it would eventually close. After about two weeks of following his instructions, the unpleasantness of nursing an open wound and the uncertainty of its healing had gotten to me. When I shared this with Dr. X, he recommended that I consult with a plastic surgeon.

I received a second opinion from a trusted friend, another surgeon who knew Dr. X. He was incredulous and livid over Dr. X's approach and advised me to immediately insist that Dr. X re-do the incision and close the wound properly. Dr. X obliged (of course) and I was back to the operating table, with another dose of general anesthesia for the nth time.

A few days after this procedure, I got another message on my machine, this time instructing me to make another appointment with my husband to review the results. I don't know about you, but for me, a message from a doctor instructing you to take your husband with you for an appointment is foreboding.

I went without my husband anyway and learned that the tissue removed during the re-incision to close the wound was cancerous. These life-changing revelations seem to happen at the most unexpected moments. I got in my car in complete shock, called my husband, and said, "I don't know what to do." I am the take-charge person in our household, but this time, he took over and told me we were going to New York to find the best cancer doctor.

I never looked back. My trusted circle advised me to sue Dr. X. I did not. I wrote to the president of the hospital where Dr. X was practicing to report this series of blunders, and to appeal to her to make sure Dr. X's practices were reviewed. I received a courteous response disclaiming everything, with language clearly penned by a lawyer.

I moved forward. My main purpose now was to get well, and I did not want negative energy to impede my healing. I found one of the best cancer specialist teams at Columbia Presbyterian in New York and went about beating my cancer.

While life-changing events seem to happen at the most unexpected moments, priorities also become very clear during these moments. Three priorities became very clear to me: our planned family vacation, visiting my mother, and getting well.

—

While life-changing events seem to happen at the most unexpected moments, priorities also become very clear during these moments.

—

I looked at it this way: While, luckily, my cancer was at an early stage and my chances for remission were high, no one really knew. Therefore, we would proceed with our plan to celebrate my 50th birthday on a dream vacation, which was a luxurious Mediterranean cruise, because who knew if we would ever get to do this again? I had to visit my mother because she was house-bound in the Philippines, in the early stages of Alzheimer's, and I didn't know when I could visit her again. Besides, she has always been a formidable source of strength.

Long before this happened, a good friend and I had a philosophical conversation about what makes a "good friend." Her perspective became a signpost for me. She said, "A good friend is one you call when your mother dies." I felt this was a moment to take stock of who makes my "good friend" list, and I decided to share with them my journey to healing. I sent them all regular updates, drawing upon their encouragement for support.

And so it was, that after one trip across the Atlantic and another across the Pacific, I returned with positive energy, my mother's strength, and the love and support of my family and friends, with one remaining priority: To get well.

I prayed, reaffirming my belief that there is only so much that humans can do, and I surrendered my fate to my God. I continued to work. Work has a way of energizing and keeping me going. My husband, kids and I all lived a normal life through my surgery and treatment.

Five years later, I was in full remission. I celebrated this new milestone with a solitary trip to Nepal. Nepal, a country of abject poverty, has withstood the tests of time and strife, through its peoples' unwavering faith in their gods, and their respectful and kind co-existence. To me, that's akin to the journey towards surviving cancer: Faith in a more powerful force, trust in the support, and love of friends and family. I still remember my moonlit walks around Lake Pokhara with an overwhelming sense of faith and gratitude.

I realize that while I survived this bout, I remain vulnerable to recurrence. I've been asked how I could live with this threat. My response is simple. You either live with fear or live with faith. Fear can be crippling while faith can be healing. I am grateful that I have survived and healed and chose not to be afraid. This very deliberate choice in perspective has allowed me to live a full and active life, and over the last ten years since my bout with cancer, life couldn't be better. While it was a major setback, it was temporary, and my life goes on, fully and without fear.

Life will continue to throw curve balls at the most unexpected moments. Be not afraid. Healing comes with time and care.

———

Be not afraid.

———

Home is Where Your Heart Lives

The word "home" conjures images of a place where one can feel safe, rest, and can simply be. It has become synonymous to a house, a place where one resides, and where refuge and comfort is a given, especially when life throws at us the proverbial "curve balls."

A natural consequence of my serendipitous career moves and my search for a sustainable lifestyle was that we had to move several times, and while with each move we felt exciting anticipation, we also knew each move came with difficult adjustments and choices that we couldn't have expected.

One difficult choice that comes with moving is the question of what to bring? What do you leave behind and how do you make these choices and trade-offs? What makes a place a "home" and what do we need to create the environment that makes us feel safe, comfortable, and "at home?"

I am lucky that my childhood home has remained unchanged. There is a sense of permanence in our island home, as it holds rich memories of my maternal grandparents, chickens in the backyard, a guava tree that we plucked fruits from right out of our bedroom windows, a wonderful wide wooden staircase where I ran up and down with our dogs and from which I once fell.

When I immigrated, I packed everything I could into two suitcases. I actually don't know if I was limited to only two suitcases. I was simply told that it was the luggage limit that came free with the ticket; besides, no new immigrant would want to deal with the complication of paying import taxes upon entry. Into those suitcases went all I could bring of the memories of my life so far: special pictures–childhood albums in particular–and some wedding gifts. And wherever we have moved since, these have traveled with us. Years later, as I returned to visit our childhood home, I'd bring back with me certain pieces of my grandmother's china, and some of her beautiful silk scarves.

We initially settled and lived in a small apartment in Fort Lee, NJ. We did not have any money and could not afford expensive furniture. Our bedroom set was purchased at a special sale at Sears; our linens and bedding were good finds at flea markets; the rest of our furniture, including couch, coffee and side table, came from furniture outlets or hand-me-downs from my sisters. In an antique shop in Hackensack, NJ, we found two old wooden pieces of furniture that we still have today: a china cabinet and a foyer cabinet. They are timeless and beautiful, and they hold a special memory of how we started our lives here.

Moving has been a helpful and sometimes unpleasant reminder of how much we can accumulate and how little we need. Parting with our earthly possessions is no easy task. I've developed a system: I have a small shoe box that contains our children's important memorabilia: their baptism candles, the first rattle, first spoon, first comb, and first favorite stuffed animal. As they grew bigger and accumulated more stuff, we narrowed down what they moved with them into one big box each, and some. The big box would have clothes, shoes, special school projects, special additional toys. The "some" contained their individual childhood collections: ninja turtles, baseball cards, skateboards and sneakers for our son; trolls, pogo disks, tennis gear for our daughter. My husband has been particular about his running memorabilia; I've made sure we have our picture albums and family movies.

I will digress for a while and share how having a pet—in our case, a dog, introduced such richness to my young and growing family's lives and helped us create the environment we'd call 'home."

Let me warn you: A dog needs to be fed, cleaned, trained, walked, and there are no guarantees of finding that perfect dog, no matter how methodically you search. Similar to human dating apps, many apps now exist to increase the odds of finding the right "dog fit." We did not use an app, and we did not search far. Somehow, over the course of the last twenty years, we found two less-than-perfect dogs that we loved beyond measure.

I've always liked dogs, as my mother had taken to having dogs in the house, and I grew up seeing puppies born and helping feed them through little baby droppers. I understood the responsibility of pet care including the unenjoyable task of cleaning up their messes.

And I also knew the joy of getting greeted by wagging tails and happy faces, and the warm cuddle of a furry bundle of life who completely trusts and unconditionally adores you.

By the time our kids were about nine and twelve, they helped me convince my husband that we could take on this major responsibility. While he resisted, saying, "I just know it, at the first drop of rain or snow, I will get stuck walking that dog," the kids and I assured him he would not need to have anything to do with the dog.

Adopt a dog.

We found Buddy, a four-year old beagle mix, at a shelter. Within 24 hours of taking Buddy home with us, he managed to gain the good graces of my husband, who became a willing dog-walker immediately–rain or shine. The kids learned to take care of this living thing; their wish was his command, and before long, they too appreciated the joy of being met by Buddy's wagging tail and happy face and his sweet unconditional surrender to their attention. My heart still warms up when I see a nine-year-old walking his/her dog. This brings up sweet memories of our young kids, particularly our son, coming home from school and walking Buddy right away. Every time our son played the piano, Buddy would sit by him and sing (howl). We knew Buddy appreciated music.

For the next eight years Buddy was our pet and reliable companion. By the time we moved to Virginia, the kids were out of the house, in college. In many ways, Buddy helped us feel at home in a new state, a new community, a new life.

While Buddy moved with us, most of our belongings did not. We were intentionally "downsizing" with our move to Virginia, and it became a necessity for us to be very selective as to what we would take with us. My husband's lucky newly married nephew completed furnishing his apartment with most of what we left. While we kept our kids' crib, it was painful to part with our children's first beds–beds that my husband made from pine wood. These went to one of the movers. During this time, we learned how gratifying it was to give one's belongings away, no matter how precious they were to us.

We settled into our new lifestyle in Virginia. We shed the big land and the big house and moved into a townhouse. And despite it being a completely new place and lifestyle, bringing in some of our worn furniture, hanging our pictures, putting on our old house clothes and having Buddy around helped to start making it feel like home again. We celebrated our first Easter in the company of family in our new place in Virginia, and with that, we felt completely at home again.

Time passed and Buddy got old, got sick, and within two years of our move to Virginia, we had to put him down. Anyone who has had to put a beloved pet down understands the pain of this experience. It would stop you cold from considering having another one.

We were so heartbroken over Buddy's loss that my husband and I decided we would not have another dog. Until we met Dude, a homeless puppy. My hairdresser set us up: she thought it was a match made in heaven and the panacea for all my pains. When we met him, Dude was all of sixteen weeks old, a fluffy black thing, weighing no more than four pounds, maybe. As he settled cozily on my lap, he looked at me with those eyes that became the first give-away of the depth of his soul, and it was love at first sight. Full disclosure: we're not necessarily big "Big Lebowski" fans, but we thought "Dude" was a fitting name for a big-spirited little dog.

Dude is now eight years old, and while he was supposedly the runt of his litter, he is actually very cute, with a pair of adorable snaggleteeth. He is low-maintenance, does not shed, is perfectly house broken, and is the smartest dog I've ever met. He is so smart that my husband has trained Dude to pick up his toys and put them away. In the few instances that he had a bad stomach and had toilet accidents, he'd literally find his way to the tiled bathroom or a smooth surface so as not to make a mess on the carpet. He is very sweet with dogs and people, and not one day passes that I don't thank the heavens for our Dude.

In the years that I worked in Chicago and maintained a commuting marriage, Dude accompanied me back and forth. Every day, he surprised me and those around him with unlimited love, unquestionable loyalty and endless joy. While the risks associated with having a pet are clear and evident, the joy and companionship it can bring are boundless and priceless. Indeed, Dude helped make my small apartment in Chicago feel like a home.

Moving is not an easy task. And while packing one's special belongings does not get any easier or more complicated whether it is packed into two suitcases or a big moving van, this is a reminder that all our stuff and the house we live in are just backdrops in the main stage of what we call "life." This is a reminder that the physicality of what we have and where we live does not make a home. When I look back at all the stuff we have accumulated and all the places we have lived, it really did not matter where our house was, what our furniture was, what china we used, or what clothes we wore.

Because a home is really not a place; it is where the heart lives. The memories recorded in the pictures I have carefully packed and moved with us–poolside gatherings in Mahwah, deck barbecues in Holmdel, holiday dinners in Charlottesville–are about the joy and happiness of being with the people and animals that we love and care for.

Except for bringing our dog along, I have learned not to worry about what I'd bring as we moved. I have learned to shed, let go, and share our earthly possessions with those who really need them.

A home is where the heart lives, and it will always be close by.

The Most Elegant Answer is the Simplest One

My life's experiences, challenges and opportunities have strengthened not only my belief that "I can," but also my faith in the goodness of the human spirit and the presence of the divine. I may have slacked off in my religious practice, but spirituality has become increasingly important to me. I believe in God and turn to prayer in my lowest and highest moments, grateful for my blessings and aspiring to serve the purpose for which I was created. Still, I don't practice religion as prescribed. I have learned to pick and choose what works for me and what I truly believe in.

My husband is more active in his practice. He goes to mass every Sunday, and I accompany him when the spirit moves me. Shortly after we relocated to Virginia, we settled on going to the closest Catholic church near our house. Unlike other churchgoers, we are not accustomed to mingling with the church community. We participate in the community worship, but don't get involved otherwise. Finding a church is easy; finding a church with a good preacher is lucky.

And so it was, that after we moved to Virginia, we found a church, but yearned for a better preacher. We heard about a wonderful preacher who offered mass in the chapel at the monastery that houses a community of monastic nuns, who make a living making cheese.

Moved by the promise of hearing mass with an inspiring sermon, my husband and I embarked on finding this monastery. After all, we figured, if the sermon turns out to be less inspiring than our friend led us to believe, our journey would not have been for naught because we would have found a new source of homemade cheese.

Of course, we got lost during our first attempt to get to the monastery, and by the time we arrived, the mass had begun. The chapel was quite small, and as we awkwardly dared enter, feeling the gaze of everyone–especially the dear nuns–one of them beckoned with her finger to come in. Childhood memories of obedience to nuns' instructions set me in auto-pilot and I walked in to wherever that finger was pointing. The Lord did not strike me, the sermon was amazing, the nuns were adorable, and the cheese was heavenly. We were in.

This is how I came to meet Sister Mary David.

The story goes that in 1987, a small group of monastic nuns set out to find a place in Virginia to establish a new community. One of these pioneering nuns was Sister Mary David. She'd later tell me that she was born and raised in Boston, the only girl with seven (or eight?) brothers, and was trained as a nurse. She was actually engaged to be married before she entered the nunnery, and with a dismissive laugh, she said, "The Lord was a much better option."

I don't know what moved me to call the monastery one day to ask if they offered spiritual counseling. Mother Superior Marion referred me to Sister Mary David, I suppose because she was a nurse, I don't know. The truth is, over a period of ten years, I could probably count on my fingers how often we met. And yet, with every encounter, no matter how infrequent, Sister Mary David touched me to my core, and gave me an increasingly deeper connection with my soul. I'd tease her and request that since she has connections, to please pray for me. After all, monastic nuns spend over half of their days praying.

She taught me how to pray, and, in so doing, to speak from my heart, to trust a higher being, and to believe that everything happens for a reason. That, in time, the reason will be revealed, or not. She was a master in empathy, always mindful of the limits of my responsibility for others. From her I learned that if I felt my ability to help others has reached its limit, it is perfectly okay to turn it over to God–as they, too, are His.

I told her that I marveled at how complete her life seemed to be while so simple. She smiled and said it was her calling and blessing to live this way; that all of us have a purpose, and this was hers. And when I revealed to her that despite my gratitude for the blessings of a good life–a successful career, a loving family, supportive friends–I continued to struggle to understand what my purpose is, she responded by teaching me a prayer: "Here I am."

And so every morning when I wake up, or when the day is going so badly I feel I'm losing my way, I say, "Here I am." Instantly, I feel the oxygen flowing. My heart opens up, and my mind feels free.

—

Here I am.

—

I saw Sister Mary David a couple of weeks before she died. She had been ill with pancreatic cancer, and since by this time I was living in Chicago, our visits had become more infrequent. I heard she was not up for guests, but she welcomed me. She was wearing a denim skirt, a scarf around her head, and a blue sweater. I complimented her on the way she looked, and she said, "I look a lot yellower in my habit."

It was a few days before my birthday, and she remembered it with a package of cheese, apologizing that she did not get a chance to wrap it nicely. We sat and visited for over half an hour. She asked about Chicago and my family and spoke about the sunflowers that she asked her doctor's husband to plant for her. I shared how I worried about what I will do when and after I retire, and she reminded me how many people just need to be listened to. She said if I had the time to listen, what a gift that could be to others. She spoke about death and how everyone would tell her she'd be fine, while she knew for sure she'd die. She talked very light-heartedly about how they (monastic nuns) go. They are not embalmed, but simply wrapped in a cloth (after changing to their habit, of course), then put in a "biodegradable box from Wisconsin" (after all, she said, with a twinkle in her eyes, she is also biodegradable), and then get buried under the ground. She half-joked about how she couldn't believe she'd be the first to go in her congregation, and I complimented her on her pioneering spirit.

Finally, she was tired, and I had to leave. I asked for her blessing, knowing that I'd probably not see her again. Her blessing was simple and precise. She said she had known me to be a caring person, and she prayed that I would be blessed with opportunities to share this more with others.

Two weeks later, I received a voicemail message from one of the nuns. Sister Mary David had slipped away from our world in peace and had left instructions to call me and let me know when it happened. I made a trip to say goodbye to my unlikely friend, who never asked me about how I observed my faith, and seemed to be there whenever I needed her to listen, smile, and softly share her wisdom. Albert Einstein, the genius who proved that the most elegant answer to a problem is the simplest one, once said, "God always takes the simplest way."

This couldn't be truer about Sister Mary David. My search for an eloquent preacher led me to a soft-spoken holy woman, who taught me a prayer that has become my mantra: "Here I am."

In my ongoing search for purpose, this simple prayer has enabled me to remain open to possibilities and has sustained my faith in God.

Here I am. I am ready to serve my purpose.

———

"May today there be peace within.
May you trust that you are exactly
where you are meant to be.
May you not forget the infinite possibilities that are born of faith.
May you use those gifts that you
have received, and pass on the love
that has been given to you.
Let this presence settle into your bones,
and allow your soul the freedom to
sing, dance, praise and love."

———

Acknowledgments

This book emerged from the encouragement of my two grown children, both "millennials." Now in their 30's, they've continued to ask me, "How did you do it?"– referring to how I navigated my life and career, how I made choices and decisions, and how I seem to always be open to opportunities to learn and grow.

I hope reading this book will help generations of younger men and women who are living through the complicated process of mapping out priorities and making difficult trade-offs.

Starting a book was exciting; completing it was harder than I thought. I couldn't be more grateful to those from whom I learned, as well as those who encouraged me to keep going.

My parents, Astronica "Nene" Gozar Samala and Vicente "Enteng" Samala: Nanay, you were the epitome of strength and courage and modeled for me what it meant to work hard, be independent and keep faith. Tatay, your love for life, kindness and generosity knew no bounds; from you I learned to seek balance, joy and purpose in what I do and how I live.

My husband Allen: you have not wavered in your confidence in what I can do and in reminding me that this book is actually important work for me to complete in my aspiration to make an impact.

Our kids, Alexandra and Philip: you inspire me every day. The answer to "how did you do it?" is simple: I kept going because of you.

The strong women in my life: my grandmothers, "Lola" Maria Samaco Samala, the pioneering entrepreneur, "Natay" Calixta Canco Gozar, the uneducated woman with the classiest taste; the nuns in my life: Sister Merita, Sister Araceli, Sister Mary David: you showed me the profound power of humility and faith; my friend Clara "Iyay" Tachagon: I would not be here without you. My "ate's" (older sisters) Edna and Aida: you showed me how to survive in America and raise kids in a bi-cultural environment.

The loving men in my life: my grandfather "Tato" Juan Gozar, you taught me there's strength in kindness; Lt. Jose P. Gozar, "Tio Pepe," you were a legend in your time and instilled in me tremendous pride for your valor. My nephew Vincent, losing you helped me find my way to more purposeful work; my other nephews Perry, Tommy and Joseph: I am a cool aunt because of you.

My bosses who showed me how to become a boss: Mr. Jose "Titoy" Pardo: I hope you read this and learn that your incompetent assistant succeeded because you taught her how to "anticipate your boss' needs"; Bob Sloane, my first boss in the US: thank you for hiring me and giving an immigrant a chance. All my other bosses, you know who you are, who took a chance on me when you very well knew I had more grit than experience. I am grateful for your faith in me, and I hope I've made you proud.

The friends I found in the Philippines, New York, New Jersey, Virginia and Chicago: our friendship will transcend time and space; thank you for making me feel that I belong.

My "Here I Am" team: you were so generous with your time, kind and honest with how I could make this book as good as I could make it: Anne Carley, Maria Coffey, Faye Gleisser, Amanda Kahn de Guzman, Maggie Haggerty, M.I., Mike Kirkman, Sophie Massie, Michelle Moshier, Keicy Tolbert, and Anne Walaszek.

And to everyone I've led, taught, and coached: you have enabled me to see how I can better serve my greater purpose and become a better person.

About the Author

TERRY SAMALA DE GUZMAN immigrated to the U.S. from the Philippines in her early 20s and built a successful career and family life, eventually becoming a leader, a teacher and a life coach.

Her coaching practice, TSDCoach, is founded on her holistic approach to empower her clients to find work/life balance and sustain life-long learning. Her clients include individuals seeking purpose and direction in their work and life, as well as students of leadership development at the Harvard Business School, Kellogg School of Management, Darden School of Business, and the Federal Executive Institute.

Terry's forty-year career spans C-suite positions both in the corporate and not-for-profit sectors. Most recently, she was COO at the Museum of Contemporary Art, Chicago prior to which she was Senior Associate

Dean at the Darden School of Business, University of Virginia. Terry started her career in the U.S. at the American Express Company in New York and completed her MBA from the New York University Stern School of Business.

Terry's career progressed while she continued to be mindful of her aspiration to make a difference, her commitment to her values, her search for a sustainable lifestyle, and her openness to growth and learning.

She and her husband, Allen, divide their time between their home in Charlottesville, Virginia and their farm in the Philippines.

Made in the USA
Columbia, SC
27 June 2018